small gardens of savannah and thereabouts

small gardens of savannah and thereabouts

Elvin McDonald

foreword by Jeffrey Eley

PELICAN PUBLISHING COMPANY
Gretna 2003

ISBN 1-58980-103-2

This is a Design Press book
Design Press is a division of the Savannah College of Art and Design

Printed in China
Published by Pelican Publishing Company, Inc.
1000 Burmaster Street, Gretna, Louisiana 70053

Cover and book design by Andrea Messina and Janice Shay

Copyediting by Gwen Strauss

Additional plant information provided by Carole Beason

Photography by Deborah Whitlaw: p. 23, p. 29, p. 30, p. 31, p. 33, p. 34, p. 44, p. 45, p. 58, p. 59, p. 75, pp. 77-80, p. 82, p. 83, p. 90, p. 104, p. 105, p. 110, p. 113, p. 123, p. 126, p. 127, p. 132, p. 148, p. 149

Photography by Savannah College of Art and Design; Chia Chiung Chong: p. 10, p. 26, p. 28, p. 49, p. 50, p. 60, p. 61, p. 63, pp. 68-71, p. 92, p. 94, p. 95, p. 97, p. 103, p. 109, p. 114, p. 118, p. 119, p. 121, p. 122, p. 124, p. 125, p. 129, p. 130, p. 131, pp. 133-136, p. 138, p. 139, pp. 141-147

Photography by Savannah College of Art and Design; Wayne Moore: p. 16, p. 17, p. 19, pp. 20-22, p. 36, p. 37, p. 40, p. 42, p. 43, p. 46, p.47, pp. 51-55, pp. 64-66, p. 72, p. 73, p. 76, p. 84, p. 85, pp. 87-89, p. 93, p. 106, p. 107, p. 111, p. 112, p. 116, p. 117

Photography by Savannah College of Art and Design; Daniel Saelinger: p. 24, p. 25

Photography by Elvin McDonald: p. 39, 56, 81, 137

Photography by Richard Leo Johnson: p. 38

Historical photography from The Savannah Collection, Jen Library, the Savannah College of Art and Design, pp. 11-14

Illustrations by Stephen C. Gardner: p. 27, p. 35, p. 41, p. 45, p. 54, p. 57, p. 58, p. 67

Archival photograph of the Green-Meldrim House, circa 1878 (St. John's Church Parish House): p. 15

Archival image from the Georgia Historical Society, Peter Gordon's "View of Savannah in March 1734": pp. 8-9

Month-to-month planting information from *Garden Guide to the Lower South*
Revised edition (published by the Trustees' Garden Club) can be ordered: Trustees' Garden Club, P.O. Box 24215, Savannah, GA 31403-4215
$14.95 plus $2.50 postage and handling. Georgia residents please add 6% sales tax.

Some of the historic gardens in this book are public. A few are easily seen as you meander through the city streets and lanes. Some are designed to be visible through gateways, while others may ask you to turn your eyes upward to balconies, and even rooftops. Many small gardens remain hidden from view, behind walls and between the town houses and their converted carriage houses. These private gardens can be seen only on garden tours given at special times during the year, or within the pages of this book.

contents

View of Savannah in March 1734 by Peter Gordon showing Oglethorpe's plan. Already the town was taking shape with four wards. Oglethorpe certainly could not have begun to imagine how profoundly this utilitarian plan would evolve into America's most beautiful city.

foreword

"I SAW DR. RALPH EDGAR PUTTING HIS SUMMER PLANTS OUT," a friend recalled over a cup of coffee in my kitchen following his Saturday morning walk. He was referring to one of Savannah's many green thumbs, a doctor down the street who clearly delights in the changes and embellishments he makes to the narrow treelawn in front of his striking Victorian home. As it happened, my friend was not aware that I was making notes for this foreword. Nor could he know I felt somewhat intimidated to write about Savannah's small gardens. My own downtown courtyard is, at best, nicely neglected. Thank goodness for the camellias, azaleas and raphiolepis that were recommended to me by John McEllen, one of Savannah's landscape specialists. Despite my passive approach to gardening, I can always count on those hardy standbys to come through for me with their mixture of white, pink and red blooms to signal the beginning of spring.

What a contrast to my neighbor! With each season, Ralph's gardening brings forth vivid bursts of color. Sometimes he includes blossoms of daffodil, zinnia, pentas, foxglove, snapdragon, yarrow, evening primrose, 'Cecile Brunner' and 'Europeana' roses, California and Iceland poppies, and some Siberian iris, too. Add in larkspur, verbena, cosmos, amaryllis, and border grass and you have only a portion of the abundance that transforms this narrow strip between the sidewalk and Habersham Street near Whitefield Square into a miniature Giverny. He does this not only for himself, but also for the pleasure of passersby. This is what is most striking about the small gardens in this book: how they can be intimate and private, while at the same time generously created for the enjoyment of many.

A stereoscopic view of Johnson Square looking south along Bull Street. Looking closely one can see bollards strategically placed to keep carriages from driving through squares.

It is no secret that in courtyards, on treelawns and even up above on rooftops, Savannah's gardeners create enchanting oases that echo the beautiful public squares the city is so famous for. Those of us who reside in the historic and Victorian districts understand that Savannah's green spaces reveal their beauty through a mixture of well-established personalities and seasonal surprises. In springtime they show off, dazzling us for weeks with tulips and redbuds, which give way to azaleas and dogwoods, then to the blooms of magnificent magnolia trees and climbing Confederate jasmine. During much of the year it almost seems that our flora wants to hide the city, as if reluctant to share her many architectural treasures. Anyone who has tried to photograph one of the beautifully eclectic steeples of our churches or details of our remarkable residences through the sweeping, moss-laden oak branches will attest to this. However, for those willing to peek through the garden gate, peer over the garden wall and look to the balconies and roofs above, there is much to discover.

Savannah is a seductive city where grandeur and intimacy are dictated by an architectural pattern established with the original town plan of 1733—the most significant in colonial America. General James Oglethorpe's design for the settlement of Savannah reflected his interest in practical organization and his hope that his plan could serve to introduce organizing features that would contrast favorably with the often haphazard, unhealthy and overcrowded communities he had seen throughout Europe. The original plan involved repeating six units called "wards." Each ward had four tithings, or areas that were divided into individual lots for homes. Each ward was intended to

By the late nineteenth century, the squares featured ornamental fountains, monuments and other statuary. Sadly, not all of these sublime sculptures remain in place, as with the exotic sphinx who once helped to guard an entrance to Forsyth Park.

accommodate forty free-holder families. Additionally, each ward had four trust lots that were designated for important public buildings like churches and storehouses. The plan also included a large open area in the center of each ward. Today these central spaces are known as "squares" and have become the most celebrated, significant and enduring feature of the plan.

The appearance of Savannah's squares has evolved through history. The lush beauty one finds today would provide a striking contrast to the utilitarian character of the squares in days past. For much of the eighteenth century, soldiers could have been seen training amid grazing livestock in these spaces. By the mid-nineteenth century Savannah had become a wealthy cotton port and Oglethorpe's plan was extended until it covered nearly a square mile. As the city became more affluent, the squares became increasingly ornamental, and before the century drew to a close, most squares had taken on the gardenlike characteristics that they retain today.

While cotton was king, Savannah's leading merchants and planters

built exquisite residences on the larger trust lots. In many instances they incorporated ornamental gardens as complements to the stately Greek, Gothic and Italianate detailing of their homes. Because of popular Romantic notions about the importance of nature, the gardens of these mansions took on central importance in the overall design. Instead of the small hidden kitchen gardens that may have existed in the back of the smaller row houses, these homes displayed and decorated their more spacious plots.

However, the majority of citizens resided in town houses erected on the smaller tithing lots fronting the east-west streets of the city. While some town houses could have mansionlike proportions, ornamental gardens were not possible. The typical town lot was defined by the main residence that fronted directly to the street, with carriage houses constructed at the rear edge of the lot to open into the service lanes. In between, a small yard served day-to-day needs such as cooking and washing. In many ways the squares were the gardens for these homes and served as outdoor living spaces for these families. This is still true

Savannahians have always enjoyed their parks and green spaces and still find inspiration from the grandeur of Forsyth Park (above). *Although these gates no longer grace the park, Savannah still possesses one of America's greatest collections of wrought and cast iron.*

Savannahians quickly recognized the value canopy provides to transform the squares into "outdoor living spaces" (above left). *Wright Square* (above right) *is viewed from the steeple of Independent Presbyterian Church looking toward the river.*

today. With turn-of-the-century croquet, Easter egg hunts and afternoon socials still very much in evidence, the squares continue to be used as extensions of residential living spaces and are frequently populated by locals with their pets and refreshments, and tourists with their maps and cameras.

With the advent of renovations and modern amenities (i.e., placing washing machines and cooking ranges inside the home), those workspaces between the main house and the carriage house could be used for other things. And so, over time most have evolved into wonderful courtyard gardens. They are small, room size—rarely larger than thirty-by-thirty feet. And yet they have been transformed in a variety of creative ways, adapting to the site and respectful of the architecture as they reveal the interests, whims and some of the personality of each gardener and owner. Tucked into these spaces are glorious refuges and places for entertaining. Where the hosts of suburbia often cringe as guests congregate in the kitchen during a party, the small courtyards in the Historic and Victorian Districts are often the magnet for social gatherings.

Savannah garden designs may be as inventive as the Tenenbaum's rooftop garden, while others are classical, like the *parterre* garden at the Augustus Barie House, or timeless, as evidenced by the Cox and Melander courtyard. Plantings are often colorful, and their values constantly change as sunlight and shadows progress over the course of a day. Many Savannah gardens are filled with the music of running water, featuring pools and fountains where koi and goldfish swim amongst lilies and other water-loving plants.

Mr. Green could be seen enjoying his large ornamental garden that graces one of Savannah's most prominent residences. Built on a trust lot in the 1850s and known today as the Green-Meldrim House, the garden still provides pleasure for passersby strolling around Madison Square. Archival photograph from St. John's Church Parish House (above).

Throughout the twentieth century, as residents left the downtown area to build in the surrounding areas, they often created gardens with the same intimacy of the courtyards and walled gardens of downtown, even when living on larger properties with plenty of land. Near Savannah, the residents of communities like Isle of Hope, Vernonburg and Skidaway Island cultivate gardens inspired by the luxurious beauty of the city. Here, too, gardens serve as extensions of the living space, just as the squares and residential courtyards do downtown.

They say good things come in small packages. When it comes to the small gardens that you can see throughout Savannah, this adage is certainly true. As with Ralph's delphinium-doused and phlox-filled treelawn paradise, they are not meant to intimidate but to provide delight. Should you find yourself in his neighborhood, take time to walk down the lane adjacent to his home. The side porches you pass by will be filled with even more flowers, vegetables and seedlings in various stages of maturity filling pots and window boxes. The springtime nasturtiums that climb to ridiculous heights give way to tomatoes that do the same by midsummer. However, the tiny courtyard at the back of the house is where many will find their greatest delight.

—*Jeffrey Eley*

walled gardens

Long before Oglethorpe's beloved squares were canopied by live oaks, the open spaces behind each town house and its carriage house at the back were service yards. As modern conveniences moved cooking and doing the laundry inside the house, the yards began to evolve into outdoor living rooms. The fact that they, like the interior rooms, cannot be seen from the street has fostered a freedom of individual expression that is unfettered by the strict Historic District regulations. These intimate,

SERENELY SEQUESTERED, SAVANNAH'S WALLED GARDENS SERVE AS OUTDOOR LIVING ROOMS

small gardens mimic the size of interior rooms. In fact, most get-togethers in Savannah include the garden. Their status as secret places allows them the freedom to be unique, fun, and colorful. It is not unusual for thoroughly modern interpretations to exist peacefully behind Federal-style architectural facades.

The Melander and Cox walled garden has evergreen and trained plants that provide all-year structure (previous pages). *The fountain can be glimpsed from the front gate on the street* (opposite).

Ron Melander and James A.D. Cox purchased their 1853 house in the Historic District in 1990. "The yard was concrete with an oval patch of dirt in the middle," Cox says. "The only planting was a pyracantha—still here and quite large."

A brand new garden was designed by Graham Landscape Architecture of Annapolis, Maryland, using redwood for the decks, stairs, and trellis and a selection of locally adapted plants.

"The back wall of the garage had to be knocked down for a palmetto palm to be brought in and planted," Cox says. "The iron bench *(page 17)* is Victorian and came with us."

Container plants like the clay window box of pink bougainvillea provide splashes of color on the deck.

The bubbling fountain is in a corner of the garden where it is on axis with the narrow passageway to the front gate, from which it can be glimpsed. It is also a refreshing presence for anyone sitting in the garden, owing to the sound of the water and the sight of the goldfish. Finally, the pool and its inhabitants can be looked down on from the deck as performance art.

The walled garden behind a house on Charlton Street in the Historic District *(left)* is floored with old Savannah bricks in a herringbone pattern, which the owner scrubs down every three months to keep free of slippery algae. The pierced upper walls facilitate air circulation and permit glimpses both ways without sacrificing privacy. The louvered door is to the garage.

Because the garden is shaded, it features mostly green and green-and-white variegated plants all year. A large, potted, fully blooming yesterday-today-and-tomorrow brunfelsia was, however, the hit of a recent garden tour.

"The garden is a peaceful oasis in the heart of the city," the owner says.

Diane and Ervin Houston's small covered porch *(opposite)* looks out on their walled garden on East Taylor Street. Dark green painted wicker furniture and overstuffed cushions covered in a muted English floral fabric set an inviting stage on a painted sisal rug. On the porch, plantings include Boston ferns, a white petunia that is fragrant at night, and an orange-flowered clivia whose bold, dark green leaves are handsome all year.

A low brick wall raises up a small body of water for aquatic plants *(above)*, with slate coping that invites sitting and watching for goldfish. The glazed ceramic pot outfitted with a bubbler fountain appears to stand on the water's surface, but actually rests on a concrete plinth. Large terra-cotta pots are grouped in the garden for seasonal color.

WALLACE GARDEN

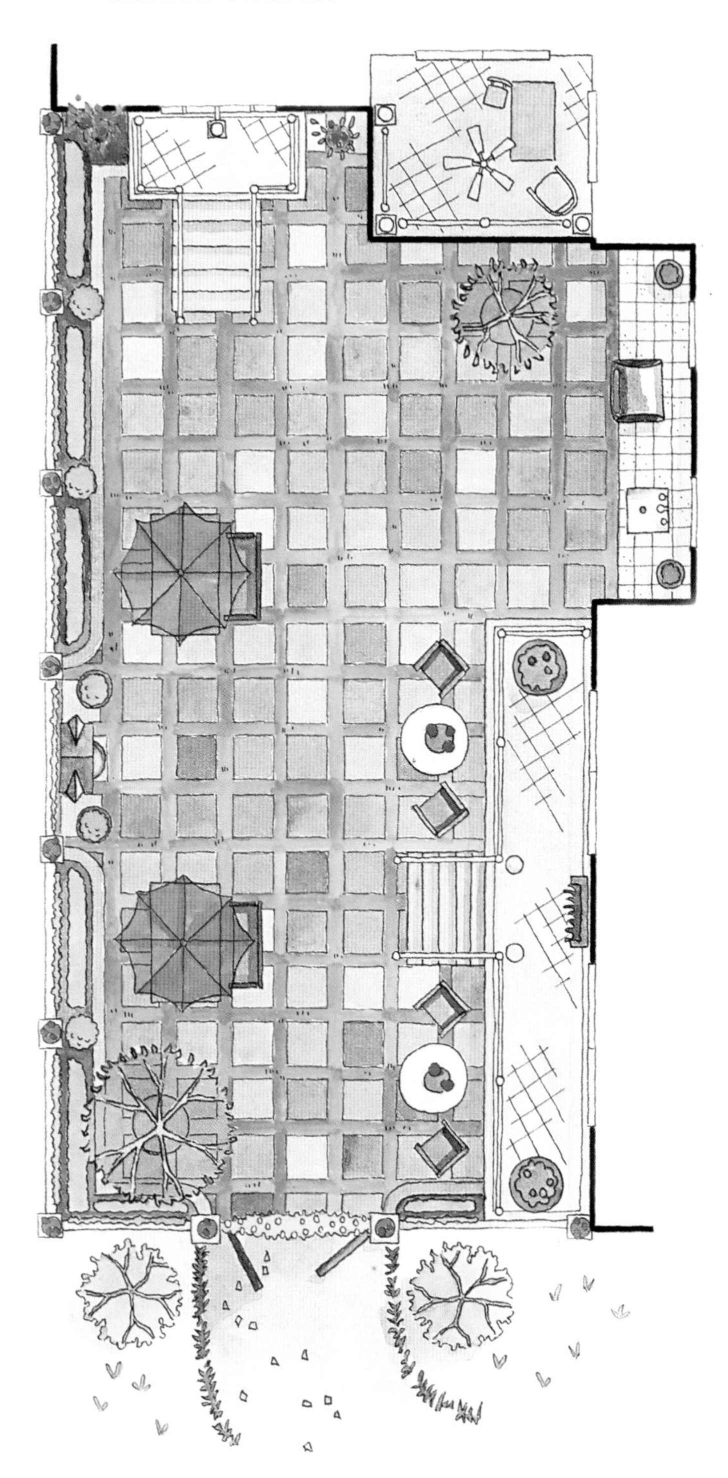

The walled garden for Paula and Glenn Wallace's home on Skidaway Island is larger than most walled gardens in the Historic District, but the siting and the intentions are the same. The garden is looked upon from two sides of the house, with steps leading down into the big outdoor sitting and dining room, which also includes a wet bar and a built-in grill.

The Wallaces are frequent entertainers who like outdoor spaces that can accommodate a large crowd as graciously as a quiet dinner for two. Wooden gates underneath an arbor bowered in Confederate jasmine open onto a path that leads to the front garden.

The brick wall opposite the house has inset panels covered by fig ivy above a raised planting bed trimmed with coping that affords extra seating, backed by dwarf clipped boxwood. The grid of eighteen-inch-square pavers assures solid footing for the furniture, while grass growing between softens the effect of a large, hard surface. The black painted benches have a design motif in the backrest that harks back to eighteenth-century Chinese Chippendale, and they pull up to dining tables with strips of wood set on the diagonal. The stair rails, while painted white, echo the Chinese Chippendale motif in the garden benches.

Rocking chairs, also painted black, are a subtle reminder of the garden's purpose—to dispel stress and nurture a sense of well-being. The sight and sound of water splashing from a cast-iron fountain that is centered between two of the brick wall pillars further underscore the garden's subtle proddings to relax. English ivies trained on cone-shaped topiaries flank the fountain, adding elements of verticality and underscoring an axial symmetry that of itself has a calming effect. Strategically placed pots of red geraniums add a cheery touch in warm weather and a place to plant pansies or other cool-weather flowers in winter and spring.

Beside the canvas umbrellas for shade, two large terra-cotta pots hold tree-form standard loquats with underplantings of low-growing seasonal flowers such as violas and forget-me-nots—an invitation to pull up a rocking chair and rest a spell.

Two professionals on Harris Street in the Historic District have only recently installed their garden, which includes a wall on the Whitaker Street side that was part of a Sinclair gas station in the early 1920s. Before that the building was a twin apartment building circa 1847. A small rectangular lawn at ground level is framed by a narrow mowing strip made of the same reddish brown bricks used in building the garden's steps and raised planting beds. The walls will soon be faced completely by Confederate jasmine trained on wires installed in a grid of squares on the diagonal.

Another wall is being draped by the self-attaching stems of a Boston ivy that has golden yellow instead of green leaves. In front of the Boston ivy are planted small-growing trees with distinctive and colorful leaves that suit them to being seen in close quarter—cutleaf Japanese maples in both red and green varieties, for example, and the rich, brown-red foliage of 'Forest Pansy' redbud *(above)*.

This garden is overlooked from the veranda, which the owners say they use all the time to take their own meals and to entertain. It is outfitted with teak tables and chairs. French doors to the dining room from the veranda can be opened for large gatherings, which the owners like to do so there is a seamless transition from indoors to out. Utilitarian iron posts that support the veranda have been wrapped with wire mesh to help Asiatic jasmine take hold and soon hide them.

A hidden garden takes the form of a mysterious, shell-encrusted grotto *(left)* that is shrouded by Confederate jasmine. This feature includes a raised pool for goldfish and water lilies.

side gardens

Savannah's side gardens are an import from nearby Charleston, where they have particular historic signifigance. Side gardens provide a way to enter the house without going through the front door from the street. Houses with side gardens are usually on double-wide lots with porches that run the length of the house. Sitting on the porch to see what's happening in your garden and in the street beyond is an accepted way of life. Most side gardens are divided into sections or rooms that relate to those

SIDE GARDENS PLAY TO THEIR OWNERS AND TO APPRECIATIVE EYES ON THE STREET AS WELL

in the house along which they are arranged—there will likely be a formal section, a seating area, and a water feature. If there is a shared wall between a side garden and the house next door, it will be either solid brick or pierced with only a few windows, thus becoming a backdrop for displaying the garden.

Those overworked words "huge" and "unique" actually apply to the live oak that dominates a side garden on East Hall Street (preceding pages). *Details such as fallen camellias on a pedestal birdbath add life* (opposite).

EAST HALL STREET GARDEN

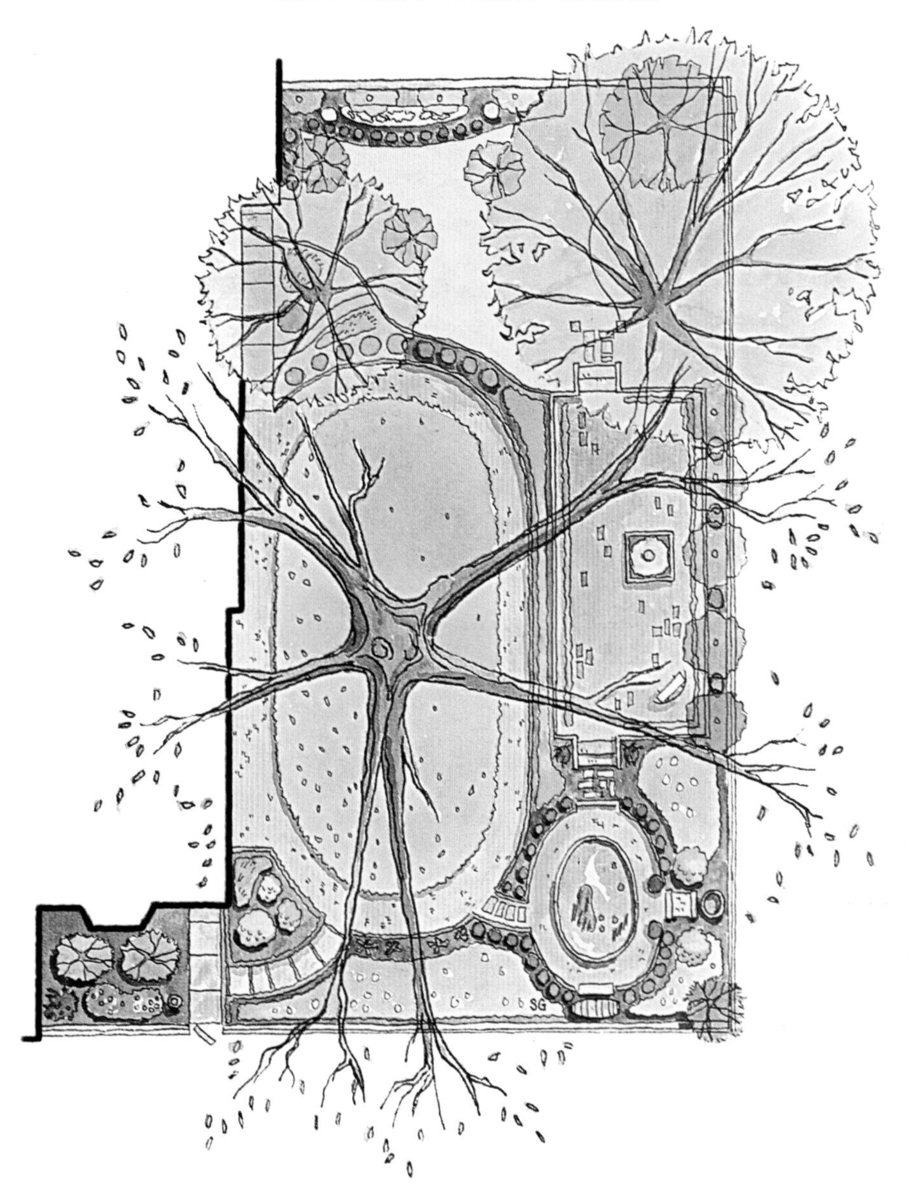

It is an understatement to say the live oak dominates this side garden on East Hall Street. Estimated to be three hundred years old, the tree is the largest in the Historic District. The garden itself, on three separate lots, is relatively new, with a brick wall at the back and in front an iron fence salvaged from the old St. Joseph's Hospital downtown.

The garden is planned to be looked down on from the side porch, hence the circular forms such as the pool *(opposite)* intended to have a soothing effect. The present owner says the garden was laid out to look like it belonged to the house, so she has kept to the original.

The color scheme of mostly white flowers and shades of green makes the space look deceptively cool in summer. Asiatic jasmine carpets the ground under the oak. Each of three beds features a different kind of fern. Sasanqua camellias bring winter and earliest spring blooms, as do the azaleas along the fence.

At the back of the property is a bed of perennials with white flowers and some other colors. "The garden is always evolving," the owner says. "I'm committed to getting it right—and better every year."

At ground level, curving paths of bricks set in running bond pattern invite garden walks to soak up the green and breathe the flower-scented air. A rectilinear terrace bounded by low brick walls gives the appearance of being sunken. Southern magnolia trees at the north and east of the property underscore the green-and-white theme.

In a side garden on East Charlton Street *(opposite)*, a wrought iron arch covered with faithfully trained climbing rose canes is looked down upon from the house. A silver-variegated English ivy spills from a hanging basket hung from the top of the arch. The ground plantings feature dwarf mondo grass in front of the bench, a massing of chartreuse and red coleus, and rosy pink-flowered pentas, all plants that manage to thrive in summer's heat. Fig ivy completely covers the brick wall, and pine straw serves as mulch.

Tabby, a cement made of lime, sand, and oyster shells, and popular in this part of the world in the seventeenth and eighteenth centuries, is the surface of choice in a side garden on East Charlton Street, with black-painted, wrought iron furniture. Brownish red coleus in big pots pick up the color from the bricks outlining the tabby; together these are echoed by the pillow coverings and behind them a pot of bronze-leafed, orange-red wax begonias. Crape myrtle trees and cycads grow at the back.

A side garden on East Gordon Street is entered through a wrought iron gate original to the house, over which hangs a recently acquired antique French lantern *(below right)*. Fences and walls seen from the street are variously clad in fig ivy, Confederate jasmine, and coral honeysuckle.

Inside the garden, there is a pond and tiered fountain to the left, and one's first steps are on slate flagstones interplanted with dwarf mondo grass *(opposite)*. The sound of the water splashing and the softness of the mondo grass provide serenity. A change underfoot to old bricks set in herringbone pattern announces in a subtle way that one is moving from the garden's vestibule into the central area of the garden, analogous here to a great hall. Curvaceous raised beds and container plantings indicate smaller rooms within the big one.

The kitchen windows at the back look out on a café table and chairs that invite a morning visit with a beverage of choice and a newspaper.

Although the garden was not planted until after the house was renovated in 1993, the trees make it appear older. They include pink crape myrtle, naturally cone-shaped Foster's holly, and the curiously twisted 'Tortulosa' Chinese juniper. Japanese maples grow along the wall opposite the house, with raised planting beds for ferns and azaleas.

Toward the back, ornate concrete pots hold junipers clipped into topiaries. Yellow lantana romps over sunny spaces in the raised planting beds and never flags, not even in hottest weather or in dry spells. Red cannas and Chinese hibiscus add a lively touch on the days they bloom, but it is the pair of Italianate terra-cotta urns with grapes and vine leaves and pineapple lids that arrest the senses in all seasons and in all kinds of light. They are an outstanding example of the role structure plays in a garden, of having objects or features that stay the same but whose appearance changes according to the season, the weather, the time of day, or the state of the plantings. This side garden shows it is possible to accommodate a curvilinear design within the constraints of a rectilinear setting, and to achieve a touch of formality in the midst of more casual curves.

The side garden for the 1844 Israel Dasher House on Pulaski Square plays directly to its well-furnished balcony that runs the length of the house and graciously invites lingering—for lemonade or stronger, or maybe a nap. When you look out on the garden from the balcony, it is a completely natural human trait to feel a satisfying sense of dominion. In a time of personal or worldly crisis, one might even look out on this space and be thankful for its expression of order and uncomplicated beauty.

At a glance this could be taken for an all green-and-white garden. But look again and you will see touches of red geraniums mixed with asparagus ferns and pale pink impatiens, along with the requisite white impatiens and pentas or Egyptian star cluster that bloom through the thick of summer. There are also leaves in different shades of green, contrasting shapes and textures that, together, form a rich foliage tapestry. Clumps of grasses, sedges, equisetum, and reeds around the pool emphasize the garden as oasis. Prostrate rosemarys grow at the front of the bed and invite brushing against to release the bracing savory smell of the needle-like leaves.

The axial symmetry of the garden builds on the statue behind a small pool with a big frog fountain that, with its splashing sounds, animates the space and masks street sounds. Four access paths for the gardener emphasize the design and could even suggest the rays of a rising or setting sun. Trees at either end give enclosure, absorb noise, and offer welcome shade. Boxwood, ferns and liriope assure carefree, all-year greenness.

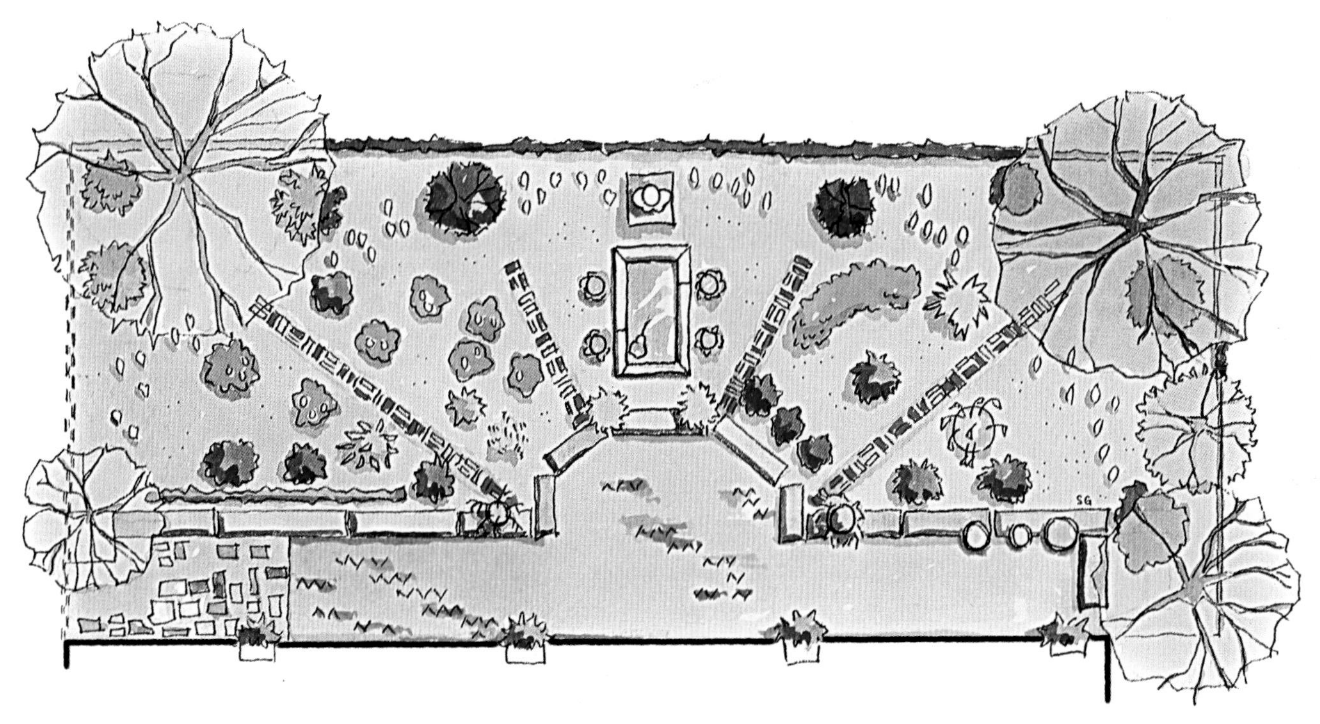

ISRAEL DASHER HOUSE GARDEN

Immediately inside the entrance to the side garden at the Israel Dasher House is a large empty terra-cotta pot *(left)*, a symbol of hope to those who see it as being held in readiness until precisely the right plant to live there manifests itself. Meanwhile, the fig ivy and Asiatic jasmine have ingratiated themselves to the point of making the pot appear more bas-relief than three-dimensional.

Sun rays appear to burst from a clump of grass *(opposite)*, and vigorous white impatiens bring light to their shady corner. Tiptoe down the gardener's access path to the fig-ivy-covered wall and look beyond into the leafy recesses of Pulaski Square.

At ground level, the side garden is the province of the gardener, who may not always see it as an idyllic retreat where all is well. This is where slugs and weeds have to be evicted in hand-to-hand combat and overly aggressive strands of Asiatic jasmine must be restrained from putting a stranglehold on the statue. To the gardener it is also a place of

hope, of new beginnings, setting transplants and bulbs in the fall for winter and spring; then, at the end of spring, setting out the heat-tolerant annuals that are best admired from a cool place—or at least with an ice-cold drink in hand. Tools, pots, and gardening supplies are stashed directly behind this scene.

The side garden at the home of David Grode and Jim Cook at 427 East Jones Street was only four years old when these photographs were taken. Having moved to Savannah from the North where he cared for more than twelve acres, Cook was surprised to find that this small garden is more labor-intensive.

He has the perspective of a newly arrived Northerner when he says, "Gardening in Savannah is different. Things grow faster, which means more pruning, and there are more pests too. And 'something' is always falling out of the trees. In the North, leaves fell only in October." A blue sky vine or thunbergia grows at the corner of the house next to a humorous posting *(below)*.

The fountain, which is more than a hundred years old, was made in England and acquired at auction "for a great price." When Cook retired, his top priority in shopping for a home in Savannah was to find a place that would "fit the fountain."

A grouping of ornamental kale and potted snapdragons stands next to the house, crowned by a Sago palm. The bricked terrace onto which the garden's wrought iron gate opens makes visitors feel welcome and gives way, at the other side and two steps up, to a perfectly manicured sward of lawn that would do any professional groundskeeper proud. Cook describes himself as "a passionate gardener, all self-taught in the pursuit of a hobby."

GRODE AND COOK GARDEN

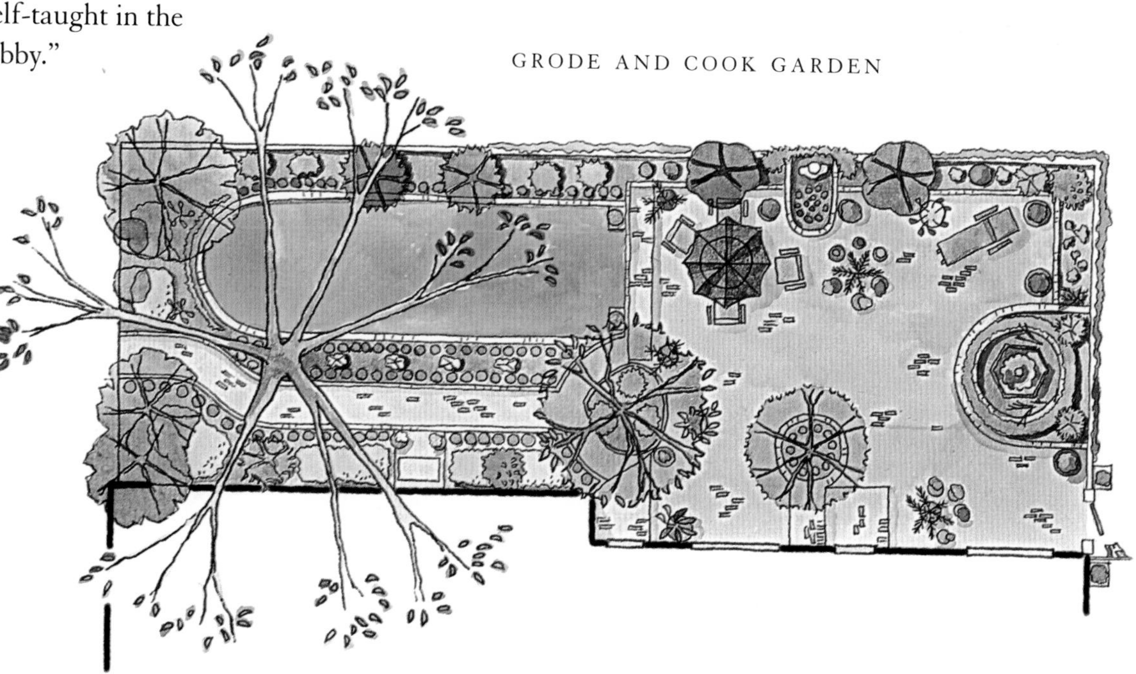

historic gardens

Historic gardens are a moving target. Individual plants live and die, gardening styles ebb and flow, and even flower colors come in and go out of vogue. Savannah happens to claim the oldest extant town garden in Georgia, laid out in 1852. And since that garden features a *parterre*—pattern planting on the surface of the ground—in the style of those set out by André LeNotre at Château de Versailles in the seventeenth century, we take that as a sign of authentic historic reference. Gardens included in this

MEANT TO BE LOOKED DOWN ON, PATTERN OR *PARTERRE* GARDENS WERE THE RAGE AROUND 1850

chapter have remained faithful to, or tried to recreate, authentic gardens consistent with their historic roots. We travel daily in cyberspace, yet a walk in the garden reminds us that nature knows nothing of Daylight Savings Time. A radish cannot be hurried through a fax machine.

James Morton's green compass stands at the side and behind the 1856 house on East Jones Street (preceding pages). *A 1960s garden awaits at the 1796 Hampton Lillibridge House* (opposite).

secured by ADT

The gambrel-roofed Hampton Lillibridge House on East St. Julian Street dates from late in the eighteenth century. In the early 1960s James A. Williams had the house moved to its present site and restored; a reputation for being the most haunted house in Savannah still persists.

Today it's the home of Dr. and Mrs. Clark Deriso and it is they who cultivate the garden designed by Williams, whose name has become legendary through John Berendt's 1994 bestselling book, *Midnight in the Garden of Good and Evil.*

The bricks laid in a basket-weave pattern throughout the garden came from the White-Redding House in Round Oak, Georgia. The fountain and pair of obelisks are Italian. Because the garden is three feet below street level, it feels private and enclosed, like a grotto. "We sit out there and forget we are downtown," Mrs. Deriso says. "We have a whole wall covered with jasmine blossoms for several months in the spring and we also have tea olive trees in two large pots and citrus that perfume the air."

The present-day plantings by Savannah plantsman John F. McEllen include, besides those mentioned already, holly ferns, kumquat, loquat, Japanese maple, azalea, pittosporum, viburnum, aucuba, vitex, boxwood, and fig ivy. Although some boxwood is English, almost all of the plants mentioned came originally from Asia and by now have proved so locally adapted that they are commonly assumed to be native. Miniature water lilies and cyperus grow in the fountain pool with goldfish. The bold, palmate leaves of fatsia or Japanese aralia complement the obelisks and together give an exotic touch.

The 1856 Augustus Barie House on East Jones Street was purchased by James Morton in 1973 and the garden, for which he is entirely responsible, takes the form of an "L" alongside of and in back of the house. He talks about his garden as having three rooms, "a perfect extension of the house." They are the sunken garden, the compass rose (*left*), and the seated garden. The sunken garden can be seen from the gate. "I like sharing the garden this way," Morton says, "because it spurs me to keep the plantings shipshape. I moved the seated garden out of sight around the corner, not so much for privacy, but so as not to intimidate passersby from looking in."

Stepping down into the sunken garden from the street, one is enveloped by green walls on either side and a simple *parterre* that features at the center a tiered fountain topped by a boy holding a fish, dating from 1870. Myriophyllum, a delicate water plant, grows in the fountain's larger receptacle, and above it a maidenhair fern has gained a roothold under the top receptacle.

Pressing on, the visitor exits the sunken garden and enters the compass rose, a sunny garden that features at a glance a rounded mass of native hollies *(Ilex vomitoria)*, but closer inspection reveals the compass points—N, E, S, W—neatly clipped into the hollies. A sixteenth-century Italian olive oil urn with Medici crest stands at the back of this garden (*below*).

Morton's newest gardening passion is the practice of training woody plants as bonsai. Along the outer circle of the compass rose garden he has built platforms at different levels to display the bonsai. Some of the bonsai, which he has purchased already in training, are thirty-five years old.

"I find that bonsai need lots of attention," he says. "They have to be watered twice a day in hot weather and they also focus the mind on a longer time frame. They are a world unto themselves, in the same way that a garden is a microcosm for the whole world."

Recognizing that some of the plantings he has set in motion in his garden could take one or two more generations to reach maturity, Morton says, "I have to do what I do with the faith that someone else will follow in my footsteps and continue the work." Joining the bonsai display is a horse bust in Georgia marble that Morton did himself as a student in art school *(below)*.

The seated garden is bounded by the house on one side, a wall on the street side, and the carriage house at the back which has a balcony with wisteria. A water oak gives shade and a weeping cherry lights up the garden in the spring. The rounded central area of this garden that is used for entertaining has a cushiony carpet of pine straw, bales of which Morton keeps at the ready for refurbishing any thinning spots. A fountain newly installed along the street-side wall features an 1870 zinc of Poseidon facing away from the sea, which Morton considers "appropriate for a port town."

Morton is an exemplar of Savannah's age-old gardening tradition, one whose dedication, perseverance, and sheer joy in the practice inspires others. A generation or so before him there was Louisa Farrand Wood, a niece of Beatrix Farrand who, for her design of the ten acres of formal gardens surrounding Dumbarton Oaks in upper Georgetown, Washington, D.C., and the execution of other prestigious commissions, came to be known as the Gertrude Jekyll of America. Garden writer Marty Ross, who happened to be living in Savannah in 1982, the year Mrs. Wood's book, *Behind Those Garden Walls in Historic Savannah*, was published, recalls that she was known as the Duchess of Terra Cotta. Coincidentally, the Duchess lived on East Jones Street at the very moment her neighbor and young gardener James Morton was first putting down roots.

Lately Morton has refired his passion through the study of Japanese gardening and his work with bonsai. He is applying some of the same ideas about dwarfing and shaping to certain of the trees in the garden, to make the branches grow down and form archways across the garden.

At the entrance gate on Jones Street, for example, Morton is dwarfing two Georgia black pines. The work is intense and slow, something that may not be completed in his lifetime. Japanese gardens have a receiving tree at the entrance. Morton's goal is to have two, which he hopes will arch together in a canopy that reaches over the wall so that "when you enter the garden you feel embraced." Meanwhile, the colorful annual flowers and foliages *(above)* in sun pockets can be counted on for nearly instant gratification.

The 1852 Battersby-Hartridge-Anderson House on East Charlton Street has a two-story side porch or veranda—a piazza to Charlestonians—that looks down on a *parterre* formed of clipped, small-leafed Japanese boxwood that was first laid out the year the Barbados-style house was built. The original plantings have come and gone, some no doubt several times over, but the design has been faithfully preserved with ceramic tiles defining the geometrically arranged beds.

While pattern gardens are intended primarily to be seen and appreciated from above, touches of verticality make walking through them more interesting. In this garden there are tree-form standard roses, and beneath them the open spaces framed by the boxwood receive late fall plantings of bulbs for spring bloom. These in turn are overplanted with winter-flowering annuals such as pansies, violas, or forget-me-nots. At the approach of summer, all of the bloomed-out plants are replaced with fresh transplants of things that respond enthusiastically to hot weather, such as impatiens and Madagascar periwinkle or vinca.

Considering its standing as the oldest town garden in Georgia, it hardly seems surprising to learn that the present owners have family ties to the property dating back to the 1850s. It is a legacy they take responsibly, first in dealing with renovations and updates to the infrastructure as the need becomes apparent, and second in pruning, restoring, and replanting the living components.

The walls and columns surrounding the garden support a variety of climbing plants that flower in season, often touching the breezes with fragrance, and softly foliate the otherwise hard surfaces year-round. These include Confederate jasmine, wisteria, bignonia or trumpet creeper, Lady Banks rose, the Cherokee rose or *Rosa laevigata*, and virgin's bower clematis. In a bow to the practical, the present owners grow fresh herbs for the kitchen in large clay pots placed strategically to bask in the sun. They have also planted cutleaf Japanese maples in the garden so that back-lighting by the sun can be fully appreciated from the veranda.

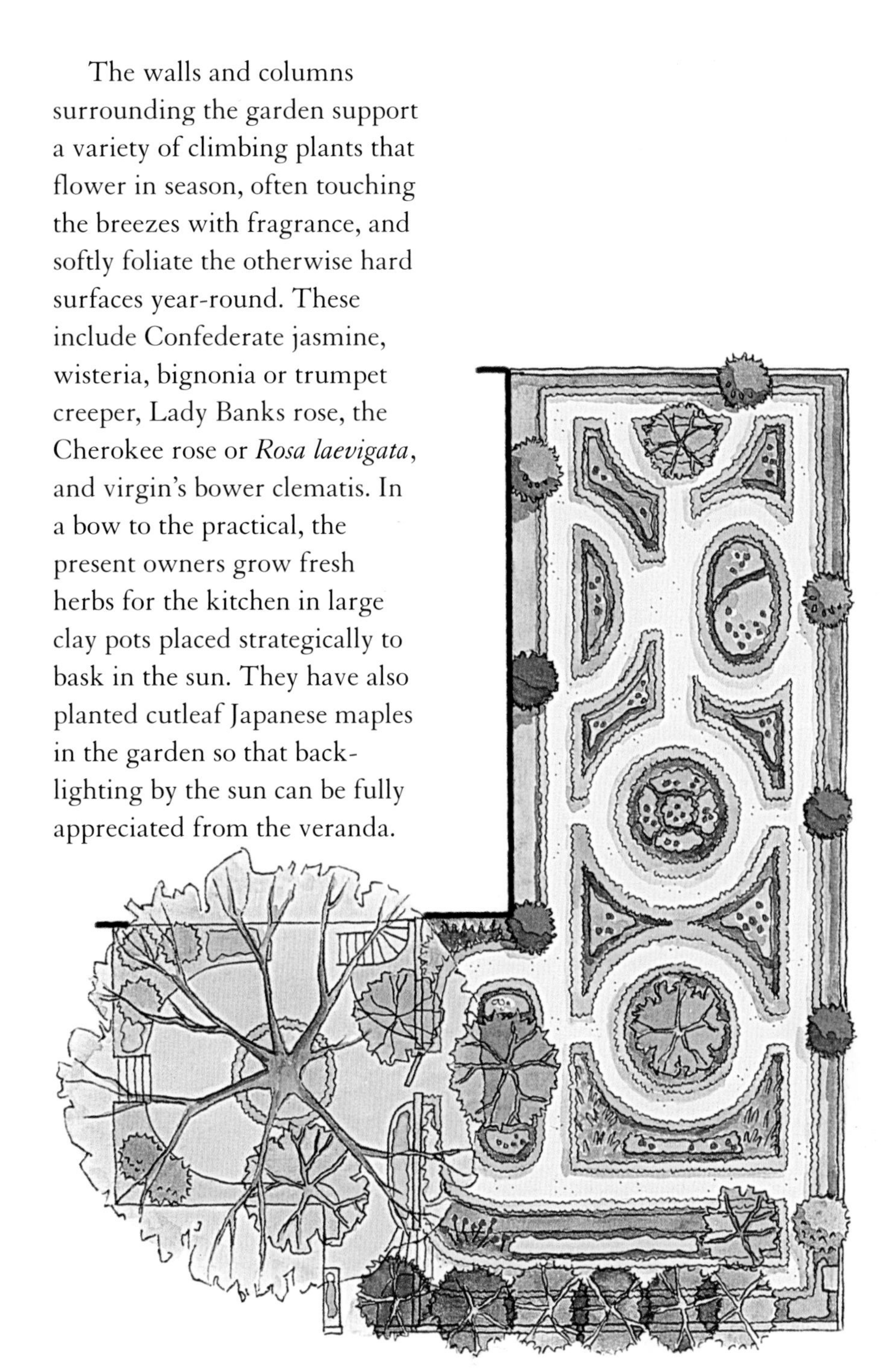

BATTERSBY-HARTRIDGE-ANDERSON GARDEN

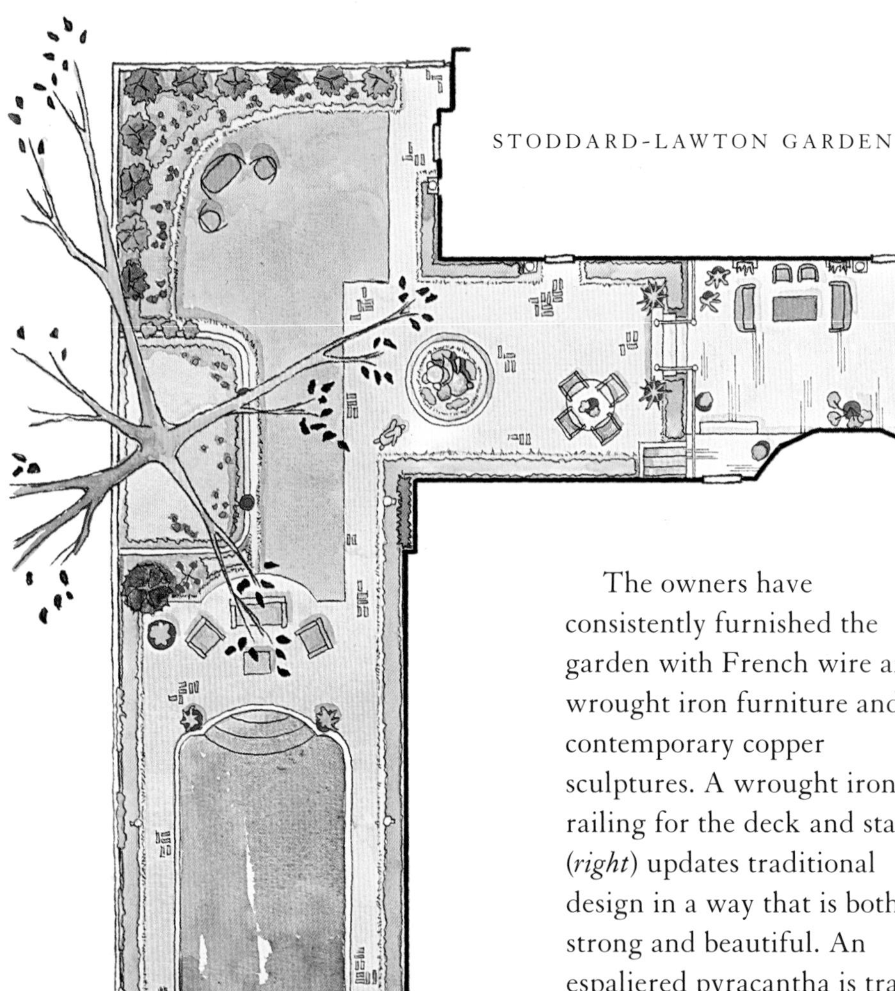

A side garden at the Stoddard-Lawton House is given over to a classically shaped swimming pool with a skirting of old bricks laid in a basketweave pattern; these in turn lead to a dining terrace behind the house from which steps lead up to a deck sitting room and fountain.

The owners have consistently furnished the garden with French wire and wrought iron furniture and contemporary copper sculptures. A wrought iron railing for the deck and stairs (*right*) updates traditional design in a way that is both strong and beautiful. An espaliered pyracantha is trained on the back brick wall for leafy green ornamentation from spring through fall and a showy crop of red fruit in winter. Clipped boxwood hedges frame the garden, fronted by an edging of grassy liriope. Fixtures set into the hedges give night light.

Instead of the more usual walls completely clothed in fig ivy or other greenery, in this garden Confederate jasmine vines are trained as espaliers in a classic Belgian fence pattern.

Masonry nails and wires form the foundation for guiding and holding the vines in place.

A table for two overlooking the swimming pool garden (*right*) recognizes Savannah romance and reality rolled into one: At the height of summer, a prime place to appreciate a garden is from a vantage point with air conditioning.

pocket gardens

American poet Robert Frost wrote, "Nature does not complete things. She is chaotic. Man must finish, and he does so by making a garden and building a wall." Even more to the point of the pocket garden are the words of the Roman statesman Cato, penned a century or two before Christ: "A city garden, especially of one who has no other, ought to be planted and ornamented with all possible care." A pocket garden can be any size of small, from a miniature landscape in a wall niche to a place big enough for

POCKET GARDENS ARE ABOUT CREATING EDEN IN MINIATURE NO MATTER THE SURROUNDINGS

seating and container plantings. The one shown here from a corner behind a town house features an old teak bench long enough for the tallest resident to stretch out and take a nap, and the pots host fashionable plants such as red Texas sage, 'Dragon Wing Red' begonia, and 'Palace Purple' heuchera.

On Whitaker Street overlooking Forsyth Park, a few simple components—pots, plants, a path, and an old teak bench—create an island surrounded by silvery marble and concrete edging (preceding pages and opposite).

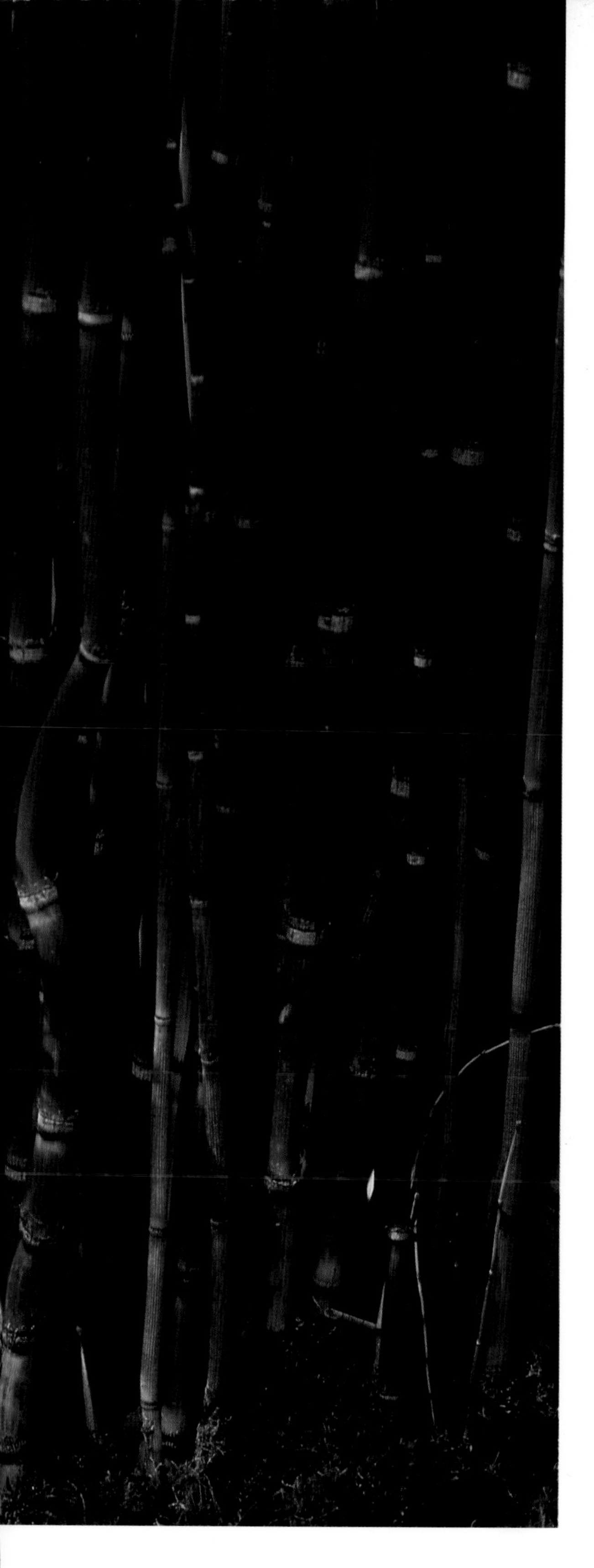

Porter Carswell's garden in the Historic District would surely gain Cato's approval, for it is a shining example of a city garden that has been planted and ornamented with all possible care. The width of a narrow town house and slightly longer, this garden can be seen through sliding glass doors from a library den where Carswell spends much of his time while he is not actively engaged in "making certain no aspect of the garden is overlooked," he says. A rectangular water lily pool centers the garden *(right)* and features a pair of lead cranes. One crane spouting water cannot be seen from the house, owing to a green screen formed by the prehistoric equisetum, also known as horsetail or scouring rush *(left)*.

Carswell has wisely applied Japanese concepts about garden design and training plants in order to gain an overall harmonious effect while accommodating many different kinds of plants within a small space. What could have devolved into the dread "dib and dab" effect has become instead a treasure trove of cultivated beauty that satisfies Carswell's green thumbs as well as his highly developed sense of aesthetics.

Bouffant clumps of variegated Aztec grass *(above)* accent two corners of the pool which is edged with winter and spring annual flowers such as pink bedding begonias, pentas, impatiens, dianthus, blue lobelia, and dusty miller. A pine tree in training as a bonsai, with stone and living moss mulch, emphasizes the dimensionality of the small space, and the scene altogether seems entirely pleasing as the setting for a Buddha head statue.

Close inspection of the Buddha statue reveals that it is displayed with Carswell's customary attention to detail. The statue itself rests on a rough stone plinth fronted by maidenhair ferns and dwarf boxwood hedging. Wood framing attached to the brick wall, together with the shingled roof, are ideas realized from studying gardens in Japan.

The garden as seen from the back gate shows its relationship to the house and the dramatic verticality of the horsetail equisetums. They play a pivotal role in preventing the garden from being seen all at once.

Alcoves and shelving along the wall opposite the Buddha give Carswell a place to grow and show his collection of bonsai, which includes several old azaleas that burst into spectacular bloom at the end of winter and signal the beginning of a new, active gardening season.

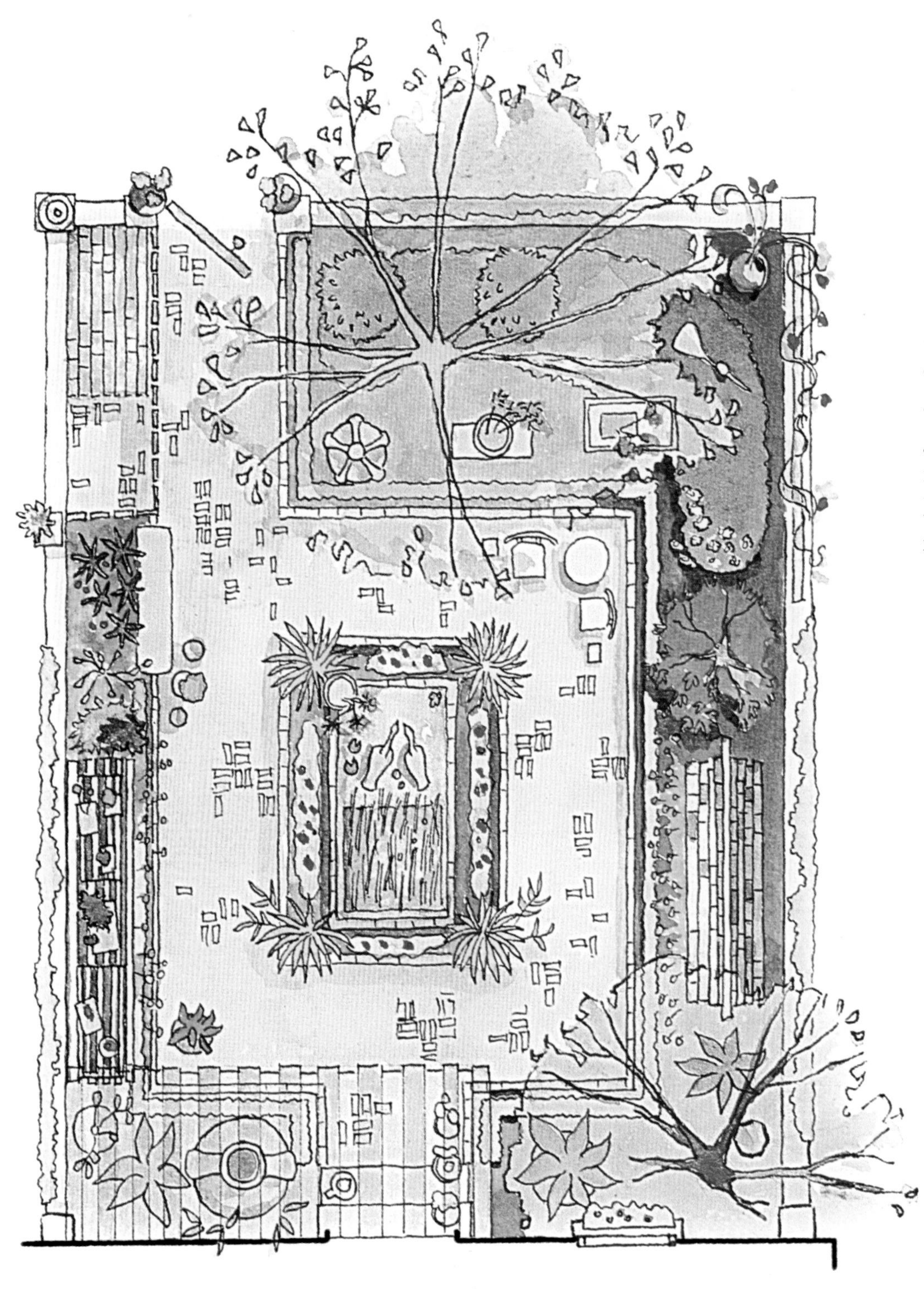

CARSWELL GARDEN

Old bricks laid in a basket-weave pattern echo the walls, and there is enough space in one corner for two chairs and a café table. Two small trees give shade, and their canopies imply the ceiling effect that helps make outdoor rooms magical places.

The pocket garden behind Ian and Debi Dickson's twenty-seven-year-old house in the Historic District is so new, the last specks of soil and mulch from the plantings had to be hosed away only minutes before the photographer arrived.

Designer Carole Beason chose to feature white Japonica camellias in large pots "because they are romantic and Southern and I know the plants will thrive in that exposure," she says. This part of the L-shaped space is seen from the den of the house, and the other—an outdoor dining room—is on view from the breakfast room. The entire garden is surfaced with flagstones set in mortar and edged with the same bricks used to build the garden's walls.

Antique pineapple finials top the pillars flanking the gate that leads to the lane. A lion motif planter hung on the gate holds variegated English ivy and impatiens.

In the corner to the right of the gate is a small tea olive plant *(Osmanthus fragrans)* that will eventually become a small tree, treasured for clusters of tiny white flowers that give their exquisite fragrance off and on from fall through spring.

The raised water garden opposite the wrought iron bench and chairs features an antique Gothic fountain *(below left)* with dark and light green mosses. Potted cyperus or umbrella plants flank the fountain symmetrically.

The Dickson's outdoor dining room can be viewed from the breakfast room. The antique clock on the chimney wall and the old wrought iron window grates are from the south of France. The sunny yellow canvas awning fits well in this Provençal setting. Old urns on pedestals hold seasonal color in the form of 'Champagne Bubbles' poppies and English ivy topiaries trained in classic geometrical shapes. White impatiens growing from a narrow planting bed soften the transition between the breakfast room and the paving.

Ashby and John Angell's garden outside of old Savannah can be measured in acres, but the Grandmother Garden Ashby has created illustrates perfectly the possibility of having a pocket garden almost anywhere. The wrought iron furniture is child-sized. Surely Flopsy, Mopsy, and Peter Cottontail are expected for tea in this leafy room carved out of a shrubbery border.

rooftop gardens

A place to garden, like a room with a view, is a common human wish. If your abode has no ground that can be pressed into service, an age-old alternative is to make a place on the roof. Savannah's rooftop gardens connect it with sophisticated rooftops the world over. And, as everywhere else, the first response to the idea is to determine if the building is strong enough to hold big pots and planters filled with wet earth. If the answer is yes, plantings can proceed, with two

ROOFTOP GARDENS LIFT THE SPIRITS, UNCANNILY CONNECTING CONCEPTS OF HEAVEN AND EARTH

caveats: no leaks allowed and no unsecured objects or plants that could be hurled from the roof in a windstorm. Drip irrigation systems and automated timers assure adequate moisture, and well-chosen plants will actually grow stronger in sometimes buffeting winds.

This cozy garden corner (previous pages) *hardly gives a clue that it is on top of a formerly commercial building hundreds of feet in the air in the Historic District* (opposite).

SAVAN

For this rooftop garden in the Historic District, it was the owner's primary wish to have a garden that would drain properly. The solution was to elevate it off the roof with steel beams. A hardwood floor in a checkerboard pattern was built on top of the beams. A drip irrigation system on a programmable timer serves the planter boxes. The gardener also had the foresight to build planter boxes at waist height so that she will be able to weed with ease even at an advanced age. Forget planned obsolence; this is planned self-reliance. The boxes are copper-lined and filled with twenty yards of soil that had to be carried up four stories. Antique tiles used around the boxes came from a previous residence and before that from a plantation in South Carolina.

The garden is year-round. In spring there are pansies, snapdragons, poppies, and amaryllis. In summer there are wax begonias, violets, viburnum, Indian hawthorn, and jasmine. In the fall the owner likes to fill the beds with chrysanthemums. And in the winter, it's time again for pansies and violas.

Whatever needs lots of sun is welcome here. A Japanese maple in a big pot is a star performer, with aspects about it that can be appreciated in every season. Another favorite plant, far less expensive, is the zinnia, especially when the weather is really hot. Creeping jenny is the serviceable plant chosen to soften the edges of the planter, and fill in between other plants, like the background on a needlepoint pillow. A glowing pink bougainvillea grows on the timbered pergola. Wax begonias in the concrete urn are an example of the stability needed by rooftop plants so they don't topple in the first breeze—or hurricane!

Cora Bett Thomas's rooftop on East Jones Street in the Historic District has all the accoutrements of a stylishly appointed sitting room, except four walls. A wood-framed canvas cover alternately shields from the sun and affords privacy. A built-in planter along the open side gives a living green wall that welcomes visiting beauties in full bloom, like the blue Vanda orchid pictured. The blue-and-white theme is established by a porcelain side table and repeated in blue pinstripe sail cloth and on occasion such seasonal blue flowers as vinca or periwinkle, *Salvia patens*, and *Salvia guaranitica*. Other plants include oakleaf hydrangea, jasmine, fan palms, and ficus for shade.

Mr. and Mrs. Arnold Tenenbaum have a rooftop garden in the Historic District that is not like any other in the world. Despite its height, this garden is actually looked down on by a much taller high-rise apartment building having numerous terraces "with a view," a fact that doesn't seem to have any effect on the Tenenbaums. They are famously at home with themselves and with the furnishings that make them comfortable.

For dining, there is a teak table with folding teak chairs set on a round cutout of indoor/outdoor carpeting placed in the center of a painted square. A large terra-cotta vase stands as a symbol of water and life. The view to the Talmadge Bridge *(opposite)* is impressive, and a sure winner with guests.

Instead of steel beams, wood pallets have been appropriated as rooftop decking. A friend suggested painting the pallets, and the Tenenbaum's gardener at the time suggested her boyfriend, Barry Shrum, from Jacksonville, Florida. Garden designer Katherine Clark, a native of Savannah, helped with the process.

Indian rain drums from Thailand that have been in the family for some time are used on the rooftop as side tables. Rocks, some with messages engraved in them—"Laugh," for example—are placed about on cushions or anything that might need some anchor against a gust of wind.

There's also a clear view of the river and the Port of Savannah. Add a minarette or two in the skyline and this could be a Moroccan still life. A white dwarf snapdragon grows in the big pot, with Iron Cross oxalis in the smaller one next to some small cacti in a dish garden. Podocarpus and Indian hawthorn or raphiolepis have performed well on the rooftop.

The trees grow in terra-cotta pots and include boxwood, podocarpus, and juniper, with some underplantings of prostrate rosemary. The Tenenbaums prefer the square terra-cotta pots for their modular qualities and the clay material which adds enough weight for stability. Arnold Tenenbaum says he enjoys going to the rooftop in the spring and fall in order to be able to relax and read in the sun. It's too hot in the summer, except in the evenings when a breeze might stir the leaves. One pathway around the roof *(right)* is made of asphalt shingles the color of terra-cotta, giving the effect of real stepping stones.

container gardens

In no part of the country has the modern-day practice of container gardening had a bigger impact than in the gardens of Savannah. When your garden is in a relatively small space, changing the pots from a dead crop to a new one is a quick and sure way to have a fresh view. At the entrance to her garden on East Jones Street, Cora Bett Thomas uses pots of white impatiens. "They look cool on a hot day," she says, "and they reflect enough light at night to give the impression of a garden." A sago palm or

NURTURE THE EARTH AND BE NURTURED, EVEN IF IT'S ONLY ONE FLOWERPOT AT A TIME

cycad grows in a large terra-cotta pot and provides all-year interest, as does the smooth, tan-colored bark of a crape myrtle *(opposite)*. Almost without exception, today's container gardeners use packaged potting soils, and they anticipate replacing past plantings with each approaching season.

At Granite Steps, a bed-and-breakfast in an 1881 house on East Gaston Street in the Historic District, window boxes and urns alternate to create a ledge garden (previous pages).

Cora Bett Thomas's courtyard garden has an arresting design worked in the bricks, a possible reference to the Chinese Chippendale influences seen in Savannah furniture, porch railings, and gates. Along the right wall of the garden there is a blizzard of white impatiens and white caladiums, both plants that exult in the heat and high humidity of the long summer season. Also among the container plantings is the nearly unnaturally blue *Salvia patens*, and a variety of white-flowered annuals such as snapdragons and sweet alyssum.

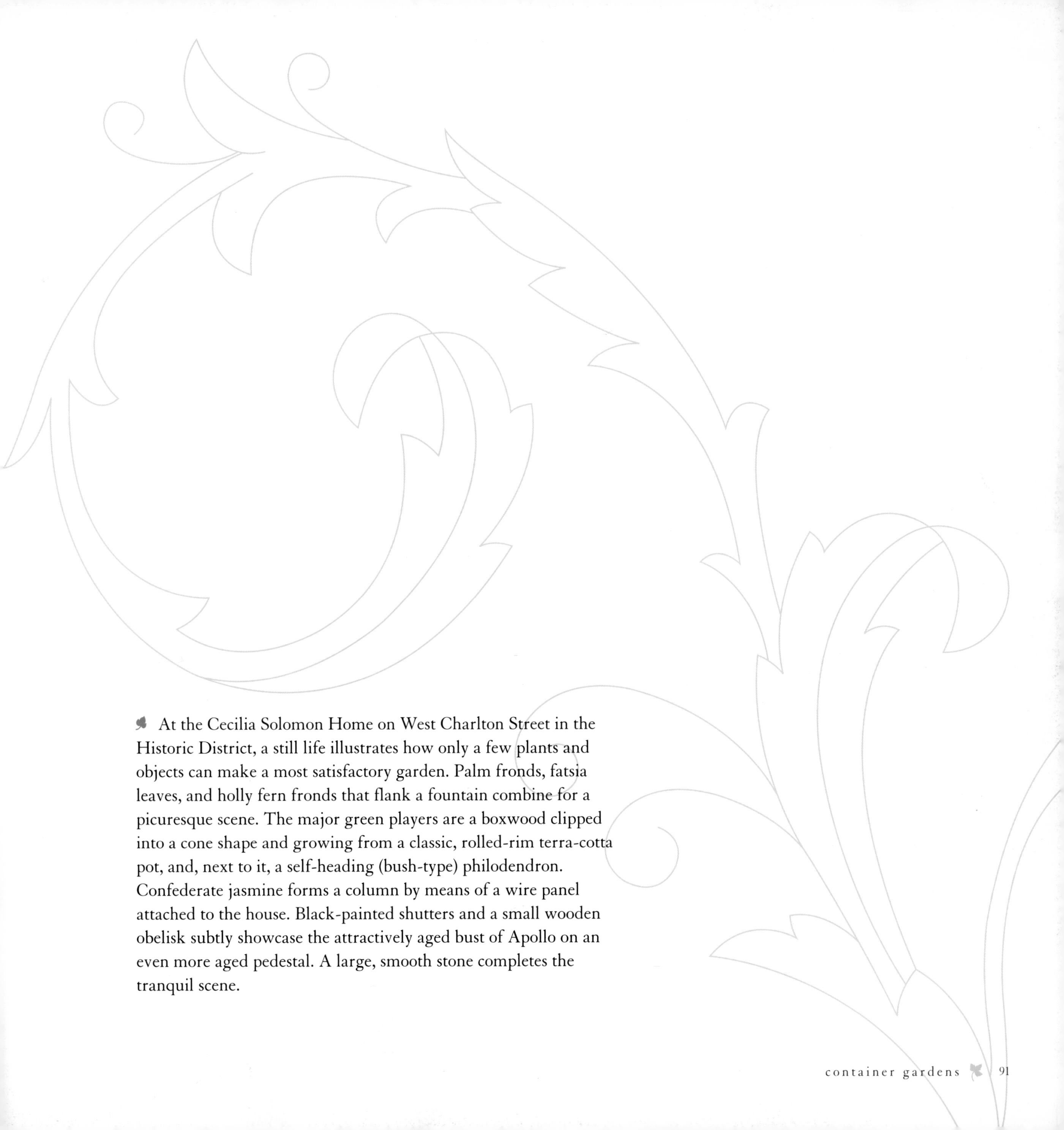

At the Cecilia Solomon Home on West Charlton Street in the Historic District, a still life illustrates how only a few plants and objects can make a most satisfactory garden. Palm fronds, fatsia leaves, and holly fern fronds that flank a fountain combine for a picuresque scene. The major green players are a boxwood clipped into a cone shape and growing from a classic, rolled-rim terra-cotta pot, and, next to it, a self-heading (bush-type) philodendron. Confederate jasmine forms a column by means of a wire panel attached to the house. Black-painted shutters and a small wooden obelisk subtly showcase the attractively aged bust of Apollo on an even more aged pedestal. A large, smooth stone completes the tranquil scene.

GRANITE STEPS
126

The cradle-style wrought iron window boxes at the Granite Steps *(opposite)* lined with coir fiber are changed out seasonally in order to keep the plantings vigorously alive. Here, at the end of winter, the upper ones feature trailing and tall snapdragons, cerise petunias, geraniums, and white sweet alyssum. The lower window boxes feature snapdragons and 'Bright Lights' Swiss chard. The Victorian urn holds the same plantings as the upper boxes. Boxwoods clipped into cones and encircled by dusty miller plants flank the front doors.

This picture-perfect atrium resides at the top floor of a building in downtown Savannah that was once a car dealership. An integral part of what is today a dwelling, its most important feature cannot be seen: In order to assure proper drainage, not damaging leaks, the unit is built like a giant shower stall with a big drain. The table was designed to feature a slab of marble salvaged from the home of a parent; the two antique garden chairs came from parents on the other side of the family.

The owners say their primary pleasure is not being in the atrium but instead looking onto the atrium in all seasons, at different times of day and kinds of weather—and from all angles. Pink-variegated caladium are superb for hot weather color. The plant is grown for beautiful leaves and there are no flowers that have to be constantly deadheaded in order to keep the planting beautiful.

plantation living meets historic savannah

Beyond all those squares laid out by Oglethorpe in the eighteenth century—most now cathedrals of shade outfitted with park benches—there is a thriving modern metropolis and highways that lead into the country. Houses with land measured in acres invite a different kind of gardening as befits the owners; truck patches are not uncommon. But, the more formal pleasure gardens near the house are likely measured in feet rather than in acres. Dr. and Mrs. Fuqua's garden in the

GARDENING IS SAID TO BRING A LONG LIFE; COUNTRY GARDENING IS THE ULTIMATE EXPERIENCE

Montgomery Neighborhood on the Vernon River is approached by graveled road to a forecourt that circles a formal garden with clipped box. Up the broad, welcoming steps, into the house and to the breakfast room, a new side garden can be seen, complete with a pierced brick wall.

Barely a year old when photographed, the Fuqua's garden on the Vernon River evokes Old Savannah style (preceding pages).

Dr. and Mrs. Sidney Jefferson Bolch III live in a restored 1847 house in the Vernonburg area. Not only is it categorically a "famous renovation," the present owners are renowned for their entertaining in a manner befitting "a true river home."

Today's landscaping has been underway about seven years, under the direction of Carole Beason, who has a reputation for helping create gardens that are both beautiful and functional. A raised planter and fountain in the forecourt *(opposite)* receives annuals, perennials, and bulbs according to the season, which play in front of clipped boxwood. Here the season is early summer and the flowers include cleome or spider flower, China aster, pentas or Egyptian star-cluster, and mealycup sage *(Salvia farinacea)*.

A wrought iron gate by Ivan Bailey opens into a side garden with both sophisticated and common plants, all well grown and all playing a role befitting a certain English cottage style—with an American accent. The plantings include a newly introduced purple-flowered plectranthus, verbena and angelonia, roses, impatiens, and an angel-wing or cane-type begonia.

At the outset, Carole found a side garden that was "a complete jungle," something that can happen in a single season of neglect in this climate. After cutting back and cleaning up, she discovered the layout for a herb garden that had been shaded to death. Carole chose to replant in "typical old Vernonburg style, with lush palms and oaks, crinum lilies, azalea, and magnolia." Bailey's gate, with fish and reed grass, leads out to the river.

Near the sheltering branches of an old pine tree, rustic garden chairs invite a visit by candlelight. There's wine, the crinum lilies are in bloom, and the floor has a cushiony cover of pine needles.

A formalized side garden *(opposite)* with gravel paths and old brick edging hosts hardy annual and perennial flowers that are reasonably self-reliant. Pine-straw mulch helps stabilize soil moisture and temperatures.

The plantings include pink-flowered mandevilla vines on the pergola posts, coral honeysuckle on the pergola, and Confederate jasmine all but obliterating the railing up the side stairs. In the beds are impatiens and hostas in shadier places, geraniums and hemerocallis in the sunnier spots.

Carole Beason and her husband Fred's garden in the Parkersburg area of Isle of Hope is full of curves and interesting plants she set out when her boys were young. She chose a fountain of a boy as a reminder of her sons' company *(left)*.

Carole is a passionate gardener who can't be satisfied until every new plant discovered has been given a try. "When I get a new plant, I usually try it in at least three different places, figuring at least one will work."

Carole is proud of an open compost area hidden behind the garden shed *(right)* where she can dump all manner of vegetable waste, chopped branches and twigs, lawn clippings, and deadheads. However unattractive it could seem, this has become her garden's source of vigor.

As a garden designer, Carole has learned by doing. "I listen to the property the same as to the owner, and strive to make peace." She is also insistent on maintaining a defined border between lawn and beds—and states that rocks are important: "They give a garden a feeling of permanence."

Dr. and Mrs. Keith Dimond's garden in Vernonburg is a series of rooms along the sunny side of the house that open onto one another through white-painted arches and gates set in picket fencing. There are ordered, patterned beds of herbs, flowers for cutting, and, in their season, succulent baby lettuce and mesclun for salads.

Outside these formalized spaces, naturalized plantings invite a stroll, with a pause to admire the dovecote—or maybe put in some hammock time, swinging between two pine trees and looking out to the river.

Next to the house, fragrant vines encircle pillars and climb lattice panels. Springtime covers the nearly thornless 'Lady Banks' with yellow roses. The view down from this porch (*above*) is to a flagstone terrace outfitted with all-weather, overscale wicker chairs and comfortable rockers.

angels, fish and frogs

Southern and charm are joined at the hip, so it is not surprising that in Savannah it is understood that at some level you are always charming in your garden. A garden fairy (*opposite*), for example, stands less than a foot tall, yet is of symbolic importance to Carole Beason. "My sons have always brought me stones from different places, and the one on which the fairy stands is from them. It's playful—and unique." Arlene and Ralph Zezza's fountain on East Jones Street has the

WHEN IT COMES TO CHARM, HOWEVER, LITTLE THINGS CAN COUNT IN UNEXPECTED WAYS

standard garden furnishing—a body of water—but the cupid poised behind a holly fern frond works magic by showing how inanimate objects can animate the living. The urn also has the character that suggests it is from another place, another time, another culture.

A cherub lolls by the pool and fountain at the East Jones Street garden of Arlene and Ralph Zezza. 'Dragon Wings' begonia grows in the urn (preceding pages).

At the Cecilia Solomon Home on West Charlton Street in the Historic District *(opposite)*, the present owner had the idea to create a mirror fountain. "I thought because it was such a small space, something was needed to open it up." The ironwork around the mirror was in the garden originally when she bought the house. "I like the mirror because when I am standing in the garden, I can see my flower bed." The statuary was chosen to be viewed in the round, "pretty both in front and in back," since it would be reflected in the mirror. "I have three daughters, so I chose the three cherubs to represent them."

Hardly a twee bunny, this Chinese warrior made of terra-cotta lives in a rooftop garden in the Historic District. The owners found him in China but know nothing of his past. The flowering plant is a modern-day expression of the Madagascar periwinkle or *Catharanthus rosea*, a plant that adores summer heat and humidity. The foliage in the foreground is plectranthus, another plant that grows so well in heat it gives the sweating gardener something to be thankful for.

A big frog lives at the Israel Dasher House on Pulaski Square, given room and water there by the present owners about twenty years ago. "We practically live out on our side porch, so we look down on the garden every day." Fronds of umbrella plant *(Cyperus alternifolius)* bring living green up close to the frog.

A wire bird lives in a side garden on East Hall Street in the Historic District (*opposite*), one of a pair the owner found for sale while visiting Longwood Gardens in Kennett Square, Pennsylvania. "I love visiting Longwood and every time I see the birds, I am reminded of its extraordinary beauty."

Potman is alive and well at the garden of Marcia and Ronnie Thompson on East Gaston Street in the Historic District. "I was cleaning up the place for a garden tour and got to stacking pots. Then I realized if there was a way to attach them, I might end up with something more compelling than well-ordered pots. The pots are actually bolted together, and now everybody wants to come see Mr. Potman."

Pan pipes in the garden of Celia and Larry Dunn in the Historic District *(opposite)*. "He lived originally in a friend's garden and when she sold the house, the new owners did not want him. They accepted my offer to purchase and now I have a wonderful water feature for the garden. We love to sit down on the patio. It's a peaceful oasis of green." The yellow flowers spilling into the picture are butterfly vine. There is also a tree rose, fancy-leafed caladiums, bromeliads, and Canary Islands ivy.

A sculpture of two carp graces a garden for a house on Charlton Street in the Historic District. The present owner found it at a local dealer's and chose it "because it was not the traditional fountain that you see in many courtyard gardens in Savannah. I wanted something a little exotic and even modern."

treelawns

The treelawn, that unpaved strip of ground between a city street and its parallel sidewalk, can be a no-man's land cursorily maintained by the city and littered by the thoughtless—or it can pay tribute to civic pride and private industry. Since most historic homes don't have front yards, they use the narrow treelawn as a front garden. On streets with narrow or no treelawn space, the facade of the building is sometimes incorporated into the design, whereas the wider treelawns permit more elaborate

DECORATIVE VEGETABLES—SWISS CHARD, KALE, RED MUSTARD—COLOR CURBSIDE WINTER GARDENS

plantings. Dr. Ralph Edgar has been gardening since he was eleven or twelve years old. "I like that my treelawn is a display everyone can enjoy." In October, Dr. Edgar plants decorative vegetables, pansies, poppies, larkspur, and snapdragons. By May, he replaces them with salvia and vinca.

Dr. Ralph Edgar's treelawn on Habersham features self-reliant plants—the glowing pink of Mexican primrose and the blue spires of larkspur that volunteer year after year (preceding pages and opposite).

A first sign of a homeowner's intention to beautify a house's facade and its treelawn is to encourage fig ivy or English ivy to cover the courtyard entry at ground level and the risers up the steps to the main entrance.

At the home of architect Alexandro Santana *(right)*, on the corner of Houston and President, a microcosmic garden has sprung up with tree-form standard roses, brick-edged beds, a cerise-pink bougainvillea that climbs to the balcony, and a fan palm that recalls the elegant gardens of his childhood in the Dominican Republic.

Alexandro sees his treelawn as instigating a dialogue "between the garden squares—because I see the squares as gardens—and my garden. Because my treelawn is directly across from the garden square, it required a response from me, which has evolved like a miniature square, with the patterns of the gravel mimicking the patterns of the city squares."

One Hundred Twenty Nine

Where no treelawn space is available, the facade of the building becomes the garden. An 1884 house at the corner of York and Habersham *(above)* in the Historic District can be counted on for impeccably groomed greenery and uniformly black-painted wood window boxes planted with all the same plant in the same color for each season—here salmon geraniums. Such simplicity and clarity of design could make a convincing argument for the notion of less is more. The black-painted wrought iron rail, window grating, and pineapple finial as a symbol of welcome are classic Savannah—with a touch of the Italianate.

Like herself, Mrs. Dorothy Jenkins's treelawn on East St. Julian Street *(right)* is a model of graciousness and self-expression. In midspring there are blue Siberian iris, yellow violas, white alyssum, and blue-purple salvia.

A retired teacher capable of riveting repartee, Mrs. Jenkins is full of pride in her treelawn garden because it was installed for her in 1999 by her granddaughter, Lori Conway, a professional gardener and designer in Atlanta.

"I thought it would be too high maintenance," she confesses on a chilly February morning, "but Lori knew what she was doing. I love taking care of it and when people stop and ask me questions, I am glad to answer if I know. This winter it's been too cold to be out. I've had to leave the garden to the Lord. I make no apologies for what He's done."

In front, cold and all, there are the tea olives, Iceland poppies, and signs of passion vine and clematis. The house was built in the early 1800s, moved in 1840 to a location nearby, and to this site in 1967.

426

public gardens

Georges Seurat was twenty-five years old when he began painting *A Sunday Afternoon on the Island of La Grande Jatte* (1884-86), yet he captured a universal truth about public gardens: We go to them to be alone with others. Besides Oglethorpe's squares and Forsyth Park, Savannah is celebrated for gardens that can be seen from the streets and lanes at such historic homes as Green-Meldrim, Andrew Low, Juliet Gordon Low Birthplace, Isaiah Davenport, Owens-Thomas, and Scarbrough House. The pink

A PUBLIC GARDEN WITH TREES AND LAWN, BENCHES, AND FOUNTAINS IS THE MARK OF A CIVILIZED SOCIETY

tulips in Washington Square *(opposite)* are treated as annuals in Savannah and mark the coming of spring. Washington, one of the original squares in the northeast quadrant, was one of five renovated by the steady hand of landscaper Clermont Lee, with Mills Lane, Jr., beginning in the 1960s.

Azaleas, some airy natives, often fragrant, and the exotics such as this pink Kurume from Japan, announce spring in Savannah with a big splash of color (preceding pages).

The Fragrant Garden for the Blind in Forsyth Park originated with Mrs. Henry Saylor, Collector of Customs for the Port of Savannah from 1954 to 1961. Dedicated on April 3, 1963, it was inspired by other such gardens in the United States and the United Kingdom, in particular the first on record, begun in 1939 at Belmont Pleasure Grounds, Exeter, England.

At the Brooklyn Botanical Fragrant Garden in New York, courses have long been taught emphasizing touch, feel, smell, and sound in the world of plants and gardens as well as the visual. Planting beds raised to twenty-seven inches height feature reachable, touchable, smellable plants with signage in Braille as well as conventional print.

The Fragrant Garden in Savannah was a worthy, valid, timeless dream come true for Mrs. Saylor and the troops she'd martialled, "a committee of interested garden club members." Yet despite their efforts, vandalism took hold, the gates had to be locked, and the site lay abandoned and derelict until a new generation

of hard-working members of the Trustees' Garden Club saw the site as fallow ground awaiting a new and better Fragrant Garden.

Beginning in the second half of the 1990s, the Garden Club focused on revitalizing the middle section of Forsyth Park. The northern end with the fountain and the southern end with the playing fields were well-maintained, but the middle part with the playground and Fragrant Garden and ruined old fort building needed help. By leading with a clear mission, the Garden Club got the city to re-do the playground. Azaleas and sasanqua camellias were planted. Next, the walls of the garden had to have new stucco, and then it was time for John McEllen to design the new plantings.

Rededicated in March 2002, the Fragrant Garden stands proud as a community effort that included, besides the Garden Club and the City, the Junior League, the local chapter of the American Rose Society, and the Delta Gamma sorority (which provided the Braille bronze signage). The Trustees' Garden Club has planted thousands of spring bulbs along with azaleas, citrus, crinum lilies, gardenias, and herbs such as rosemary. But the most important thing they have done is to form an endowment to maintain the garden.

The Pei Ling Chan Garden for the Arts is a SCAD—Savannah College of Art and Design—response to a formerly vacant lot on Martin Luther King Boulevard. Work began in the spring of 1996; the site was dedicated in November of that year and named for the generous support of the Pei Ling Chan Charitable Trust.

The project represented a collaboration between the college's architecture and foundation studies departments, under the supervision of Emad Afifi and Maureen Garvin. Students created designs for the garden, which were juried by faculty members. Four students had their designs selected: Meredith Long, Christian Sottile, Jeff Stein and Amy Verlinden. Students in a color theory course created color and plant schemes; the rosy red-leafed loropetalum pictured here is an example of their vision.

In keeping with the cultural diversity of the SCAD community, the garden is divided into sections representing different garden traditions around the world. The Frances Helms Clinard English Garden features winding paths, a pond, and exuberant blooming borders characteristic of the traditional cottage style garden *(opposite)*. The S. C. Chan Asian Garden *(right)*, named for the wife of Pei Ling Chan, features a Zen landscape of raked gravel and rocks. The Lela Goldson African-American Garden has indigo and blueberry bushes. The French Garden *(page 133)* is a formal geometric design.

Architecture students designed the garden and also translated their plans into practical terms to actually build the structures.

Afifi says of the garden today, "The design is smart and clever and innovative and metaphorical. The square fence represents the square grid system of Savannah, yet what is inside the grid is diverse, unusual, creative. The garden represents the way SCAD is part of the city. And today when the architecture department holds a design charette they begin it in the garden, to show the students how ideas can become reality."

The formal garden behind the Granite Steps Inn on East Gaston Street in the Historic District *(opposite)* has been recently installed. The main design, worked with boxwood hedging and privet topiaries, can be appreciated as a viewing garden from above, or as a place to walk around or to sit. Cotton money built the house in 1881, but notoriety has come from the more recent days of art dealer James Williams, whose life was put out for all to read in "The Book," local shortspeak for *Midnight in the Garden of Good and Evil*, published in 1994. Today there is nothing even vaguely suspicious about any of the gardens at the Granite Steps. In fact, the Inn is open daily from eleven to four for the public to visit, inside and out.

A side garden *(above)* at the Gastonian Inn can be seen from both the street and the lane. Azaleas, boxwood, dusty miller, and bedding begonias form ranks, by height, that flank the central lawn and fountain.

work spaces

Early in Gertrude Jekyll's writings, before 1900, she noted that people were apt to frustrate their gardeners by not providing them a proper work table for potting and propagating. Half a century later, America's sweetheart garden designer, Thomas Church, implored would-be new gardeners entering the vast fields of new houses after World War II to sensibly set aside part of the yard to be a home nursery and garden center. Surely Jekyll and Church would smile on these practical Savannah gardeners who

EVERY GARDENER NEEDS A PLACE TO POT,
THE SAME AS EVERY COOK NEEDS A KITCHEN

make sure they have everything needed to work. Here, a small garden house has tiers of grow-lighted shelves for starting rare seeds and multiplying scarce plants from cuttings. A corrugated fiberglass roof filters sunlight on winter days when the room is filled with potted tropicals brought in from outdoors.

Carole Beason stores clean clay pots by size, and manages to have them be both attractive and handy (preceding pages).

Outside Carole Beason's home in summer *(previous page)*, the lawn is edged "to the nines" next to a grassy low hedging of liriope. A dwarf citrus that lives in a tub appears ready to harvest.

Another outbuilding with a breezeway connecting it to the garage is used to store large gardening equipment and extra supplies such as packaged potting mixes. Often-used garden tools with medium to long handles are stored business-end up in a large terra-cotta pot. Gardening gear, topiary frames awaiting their turn to host English ivies, and a weather indicator are arranged on hooks attached to the wall.

"I tend to tidy the place after each major foray of work," Carole says. "I've learned it's a mistake to think you do not have time to neaten your work table or potting bench before you start a new project." Another way she helps maintain a tidy garden workplace is occasionally to remind herself of a saying copied from a needlepointed pillow: *Don't put it down; put it away.*

At the Fuqua's in the Montgomery Neighborhood on the Vernon River, Carole Beason designed a classic white-painted pergola to define an outdoor dining room. The old bricks are laid in a herringbone pattern. Along the far side, against the brick wall, is a double sink, a work counter, and a grill. At the back of the space, against the garage wall, is a painted black screen to provide privacy for an outdoor shower.

"I've raised a family," Carole says, "and I know how convenient and wonderful it can be to hose down a space that has been invaded by beach sand and crumbs, to name a couple of possibilities. Having a shower outdoors is a great convenience after a day of gardening and it keeps a lot of potential mud and grit out of the house."

Mrs. Ashby Angell is a dedicated, full-time gardener who moved to this property over twenty years ago. She is known as the flower lady who grows lots of annual and perennial flowers in her country garden and permits others who do flowers for their churches to come and pick as the need arises.

The little greenhouse is used for starting seeds in the spring, but mostly through the cold weather as a winter garden where she can coddle her favorite tropicals and succulents such as subtly colored echeverias and the ghostly graptopetalum. Begonias and cymbidium orchids also spend the coldest months indoors, along with maidenhair ferns, bromeliads, ponytail palm or beaucarnea, and unusual ficus.

Dr. and Mrs. Sidney Jefferson Bolch III wanted a greenhouse for their orchids that would have architecture appropriate to their 1847 house in the Vernonburg area. It was built tall enough to fit the proportions of the house and match the elegant style. The base walls are tabby, as are the structural pillars of the main house. A wisteria is in training to come up along the eaves of the greenhouse and provide much needed shade. The doors to the greenhouse were original to the main house.

A sink inside facilitates cleaning orchid plants before placing them on display in the house and also assists in maintaining a beginning collection of bonsai.

SMB

Working long hours at a potting bench can get lonely, but not with this life-size cowboy, created by a wood carver in Oregon. The owner of this rooftop garden work center and home nursery found the cowboy while traveling in the Pacific Northwest and had him shipped home to Savannah in a pine box.

Note the industrial lighting fixtures, and in particular the one that is located over the potting bench and outdoor sink. If a gardener has good electric light, it's often possible to do potting, seed planting, and cutting propagation at night, as convenient, and for the potentially calming effect these activities have.

must-have plants for the southern garden

Many of these plants were chosen for their fragrance, their ability to add color year-round, or their hardiness in the Savannah area.

trees and shrubs

Abelia (*Abelia floribunda*), an easy-to-grow, medium-size hedge. Bronze foliage in the winter. Small pinkish white flowers in June that attract butterflies.

Azaleas (*Rhododendron hybrida*) are one of the most popular and easily grown shrubs in Southern gardens. Thrive in filtered light or wooded areas beneath tall pine or oak trees.

Banana Shrub (*Michelia figo*), a large shrub with banana-scented, creamy-white flowers.

Beautyberry (*Callicarpa bodinieri*), a large, fast-growing shrub native to Savannah. "Outrageous" purple berries in October and November. Drought-resistant.

Camellia with its waxy, dark green leaves is perfect for the South. Prefers semishade under pine trees. Provides wonderful blossoms in a wide range of color throughout winter. Both *Camellia japonica* and *Camellia sasanqua* thrive in the area. The *japonica* variety are good for cuttings; the blossoms can be floated in water for lovely fragrance indoors. The *sasanqua* variety cannot be used for cuttings but is valuable in landscaping as it forms good hedges and will espalier.

Chinese Witchhazel (*Loropetalum chinense*), a large shrub to small tree that likes sun to partial shade. Beautiful burgundy foliage. Pink flowers bloom at the end of winter.

Daphne (*Daphne odora*) loves eastern exposure with partial sun. Worth the trouble for its fragrant blossoms.

Fatsia, large, dark green, dramatic leaves add texture to the garden.

Forsythia, lovely vibrant yellow blossoms in the early spring.

Flowering Quince (*Chaenomeles speciosa*) loves sun to partial shade. Good in borders and wonderful for color. Pest-free. Flowers in early spring.

Gardenia, fragrant waxy white flowers in early summer.

Hydrangeas of the oak-leaf type are native to the Savannah area. Hydrangeas in general do well, especially 'Nikko Blue' and 'French Lace Cap.' There is also a climbing variety, 'Moonlight,' which assists in vertical gardening.

Japanese Maple (*Acer palmatum*), red leaves that provide vibrant color and accent. The more serrated the leaves, the more dwarfed the tree will be.

Carolina Jasmine (*Gelsemium sempervirens*) is a woodsy climbing shrub with bright yellow blossoms.

Confederate Jasmine (*Trachelospermum jasminoides*) has white flowers, grows well and blooms profusely in Savannah in the spring. Easily trained to cover fences, walls, or to climb a trellis.

True Jasmine (*Jasminum sambac*), or 'Maid of Orleans,' blooms all through warm weather.

Royal Star Magnolia (*Magnolia stellata*) is a small tree with large, fragrant white blooms in early spring.

Satsuma Citrus can be grown in the ground or in a container. Wonderful fruit. Nice, fragrant blooms.

Spreading Yew (*Cephalotaxus prostrata*) thrives in mild to deep shade. Large, spreading needles make a nice contrasting foliage. Deer-resistant.

Sweet Shrub (*Calycanthus floridus*) is a native, medium-size shrub with fragrant, purplish-brown, inconspicuous flowers in the spring.

Tea Olive (*Osmanthus fragrans*), also called sweet olive, is a large shrub to small tree. Delightfully, uniquely fragrant, very small, creamy-white flowers bloom from October to January and often to the end of spring.

odd and rare

Carrion Flower or **Starfish Cactus** (*Stapelia gigantea*), perennial succulent with toothy stems and large flowers shaped like starfish, which give off a knee-bending stench.

Night-blooming Cereus is a spectacular nocturnal bloomer with individual flowers the size of a dinner plate that last only one evening, but a mature plant may bloom on and off all summer.

Orchid Cactus (*Epiphyllum*) flowers well when pot- or hanging-basket-bound. The long, straplike branches bear large, showy funnel-shaped flowers. As a rain forest native, it appreciates the high humidity in Savannah's gardens.

Pitcher Plant, or **Nepenthes,** likes the high humidity of the Savannah region. It produces hollow, pitcher-shaped flowers, hence "pitcher plant."

Queen's Tears (*Billbergia nutans*), also known as "friendship plant." Bromeliad with exotic colorful blossoms in March. Divide after it blooms and share with friends. Other bromeliads as available can provide exciting color during the warm months in a mostly shaded part of the garden.

Sunrise Cactus or **Easter Cactus** (*Rhipsalidopsis gaertneri*) blooms in April and May. Opens with the sun and closes at night.

bulbs, rhizomes, and tubers

Many bulbs will grow in the Savannah area if treated as annuals and replanted each year. These include **tulips, anemones,** and **hyacinths.** (See note in Twelve Month Planting Guide about refrigerating tulips.) **Daffodils, amaryllis,** and **paper-white narcissus** don't require the colder temperatures and may return year after year.

Daylily (*Hemerocallis*) thrives in any soil with sun to partial shade. Different varieties bloom from spring to fall.

Ginger Lily (*Zingiberaceae*) loves full sun. Wonderfully fragrant late summer bloom. Other "lilies" that grow well are **Butterfly Lily** (*Hedychium flavescens*) and **Pinecone Lily** (*Zingiber zerumbet*).

Gloxinia Bolivian Sunset (*Gloxinia sylvatica*), a tropical perennial that produces an abundance of red tubular flowers. Drought tolerant when established.

Parrot Lily (*Alstroemeria psittacina*) can be invasive, but the dark red tubular blooms in June are worth the effort to keep the plants under control.

Rain Lily (*Zephyranthes atamasco*) likes sun or shade. White flower in early spring. Blooms following the rain. *Zephyranthes grandiflora* blooms in late summer with pink flowers.

Toad Lily (*Tricyrtis*) is a perennial that thrives in part sun to part shade. Foliage is perfect for borders. Blooms in the fall with clusters of pink, orchidlike flowers.

annuals

Coleus (*Solenostemon*) has undergone tremendous improvements in recent years. The cutting-propagated cultivars sold for sun to part shade are outstanding for hot-weather color from the leaves. An heirloom variety known as 'Purple Duck Foot' is sterile, never blooms, but always makes a handsome ground cover for large containers or as bed edging.

Dianthus is great for rock gardens. All kinds grow well in this area.

Johnny Jump-up (*Viola tricolor*) comes in many colors, including nearly black, and transplants can be set in the fall or seeds sown after summer heat abates. Blooms in warm spells through winter and all through spring.

Pansy (*Viola tricolor*) is the "big sister" of Johnny Jump-up and has the same growth cycle. Set out transplants in the fall, or sow seeds after summer heat abates. Blooms in warm spells all winter and until summer heat knocks out the plants and they can be replaced with summer annuals.

Petunia and the closely related **Calibrachoas**, especially the type known as 'Million Bells,' are wonderful summer bloomers when planted in containers.

Sweet Pea (*Lathyrus odoratus*) needs to be planted from seed in October in full sun for blossoms all spring.

perennials

Cast Iron Plant (*Aspidistra elatior*) has dark green, wide-bladed leaves for bold-textured ground cover. Thrives in shade. Very tolerant of all conditions and spreads readily.

Lantana has naturalized in the Savannah area. Blooms from summer to frost. The newer sterile cultivars that do not set seeds bloom the most and also won't become weedy.

Ligularia has large rounded leaves, often yellow spotted, hence 'leopard plant.' A good border or bedding plant. Yellow, fall-blooming flowers.

Phlox is good for bedding. Versatile, grows extremely well in this area. Blooms from spring to frost.

Sedums of all types thrive in the Savannah area.

Stoke's Aster (*Stokesia leavis*) is native to the Savannah region. Grows in light sandy soil. Outstanding perennial and good border plant.

Violet (*Viola*), of which there are many native and naturalized varieties, are useful in gardens, especially as ground cover in shade that is likely to be dry in hot weather.

herbs

All kinds of **mint** will grow in the Savannah area, including chocolate, orange, and peppermint. **Rosemary** can be used as a border or in pots or raised planting beds. Many varieties of **sage** grow well, and **pineapple sage** (*Salvia elegans*) has brilliant red flowers until frost. **Oregano** does well, as does **dill** in full sun, **parsley**, **Spanish lavender**, and **lemon balm**.

twelve month planting guide

JANUARY

January is the time to get a head start on spring.

Begin planting and transplanting trees and shrubs. To lessen the shock of transplanting, large shrubs and small trees should be root pruned. With a shovel, carve a circle about a foot deep and twenty-four to thirty-six inches from the trunk all the way around the plant. Transplant six to twelve months later when hair roots have developed.

Tulips can be planted. They should have been in the refrigerator for two months prior to planting. But when storing bulbs in the refrigerator, avoid sharing the space with fruit and vegetables because they give off ethylene gas, which will neuter the bulbs. Daffodils may still be planted. Sow seeds of herbs. Vegetable seeds that may be sown outside are: English peas, edible pea pods, collards, spinach, lettuce, leeks and mustard. Sow seeds of carrots and beets in late January. Put out broccoli, brussels sprouts, cauliflower plants and onion sets now or in early February.

Throw coffee grounds on acid-loving plants like azaleas and camellias. Prepare beds with lime, organic material, and fertilizer. Pull seedling trees from beds.

In case of a hard freeze, place Spanish moss over pansies and other tender plants.

FEBRUARY

Trees and shrubs should be planted now.

Flowering plants, both annuals and perennials, may be put in the ground. Roses should be planted. Rapid maturing, cool-season vegetables such as lettuce, garden peas, radishes, carrots, spinach, mustard and potatoes may still be sown outside this month.

February is a good month for pruning. Vitex, crape myrtle and others that bloom in summer should be pruned now. Prune out old canes in oleander. Prune camellias. Prune spring flowering plants such as azalea, spirea and dogwood after they have bloomed.

Fertilize shade and flowering trees.

MARCH

March is a busy gardening month. The average last frost date for the coastal area is March 15.

Summer blooming annuals such as zinnias, portulaca, salvia and cleome may be started from seed inside and put out at the end of the month as it begins to warm. Sow nasturtiums in poor soil and full sun.

Zinnia seeds may be sown at intervals until August for bloom and cut flowers into the fall. Petunias, lantana and hollyhock may be put into the ground when danger of frost is over. Perennial bedding plants may be put out. Plant summer flowering or foliage-type bulbs and tubers. These varieties include canna, gloriosa lily, tulbaghia, agapanthus, montbretia and gladiola.

Cool-season vegetables may still be planted, but it is also time to plant summer vegetables such as corn, beans and squash.

Complete heavy pruning begun in February. Delay pruning of azaleas and spring blooming shrubs until after they have bloomed.

Fertilize shrubs, trees, ground covers and vines this month, again in May, and again in July.

Spray dogwoods with a fungicide. You may want to spray shrubs and trees with a dormant spray. Roses may be sprayed or dusted every ten days during the growing season. Treat your lawn with herbicide.

APRIL

Many types of flowers can be planted this month.

Plant warm-season annuals, perennials, shrubs and trees. Heat-loving zinnia, marigold, portulaca, rudbeckia, gloriosa daisy and celosia may be sown where they are to grow. Plants from garden centers may be planted. Zinnias may be planted each month through July for continual blooms until the first frost. Shade-loving plants such as begonias, impatiens, ageratum and phlox can be planted among ferns and hostas. You will have bushier, stronger plants if you pinch off all blooms and buds from the new plants at planting time. Chrysanthemums should be rooted and replanted or divided.

Dahlias and canna lilies may be planted this month. Dahlias can be planted through June for continual blossoms. Continue planting gladiola every two weeks until the end of July for cut flowers into the fall.

Put out tomatoes, eggplant, squash, cucumbers and other summer vegetables. Plant basil, dill and other annual herbs. Start hanging baskets and pots for your patio or porch.

Prune azaleas after they have bloomed.

Water everything well unless rainfall is adequate.

MAY

As the weather warms, planting slows down.
Care and feeding become the gardening focus.

Warm weather annuals may still be planted for summer color. Daylilies are beginning to bloom. Caladium tubers may be planted at this time. For autumn blooms, plant already rooted chrysanthemums.

Plant warm-weather vegetables such as beans, squash, tomatoes, melons and eggplant if not planted in April. Plant okra summer peas and butter beans.

Prune spring-flowering shrubs as soon as blooms fade. Azalea pruning must be completed because flowers will begin to set in July for next spring.

Fertilize shrubs and trees for the second time since March. Annuals and perennials need regular fertilization every four to five weeks. Crape myrtle needs fertilizer, as do gloriosa lilies and roses.

Keep your eyes out for insects such as lace bugs, spider mites, and aphids. Spray or dust as needed. With high humidity, fungal diseases may become a problem. They can be controlled with fungicide. Look for lawn diseases on St. Augustine and centipede. Brown patch is apt to appear at this time of year.

If there is not enough rain, water your beds and lawn well once a week, applying at least one half to one inch of water. To conserve moisture and decrease weeds, be sure to mulch shrubs and flowers.

JUNE

Enjoy the harvest of most vegetables.

Remove spent blossoms on annual flowering plants as much as possible.

Prune out tips of chrysanthemums and dahlias every three weeks until August for bushier growth and more blooms.

Yellow leaves on azaleas may indicate nutrient deficiency. Your county extension agent can perform a soil sample test to discover what treatment your soil needs.

Spray or dust as needed for white flies, aphids, downy mildew, lace bug and scale. Mole crickets in your lawn may become evident this month.

Continue to water weekly if there is not enough rain. Complete mulching of beds with pine straw.

JULY

Plant your second crop of summer vegetables.
Tomatoes, squash and summer peas may still be planted.

Remove dying flower heads and cut back leggy annuals, especially salvia. Cut back herbs. Continue to pinch back the growing tips of your chrysanthemums. Buds for next year's blooms on azaleas will set in July, so pruning should be completed.

Fertilize annuals every four to five weeks. Give shrubs their last fertilization of the season.

Watch for insects on vegetables and flowers.

Fertilize your lawn this month. Raise cutting mower one half to one inch to keep the roots cooler and conserve moisture.

Keep vegetable and flower beds weeded and mulched. Water regularly and adequately.

AUGUST

Since August days are too hot for extensive outdoor gardening,
plan to do what is necessary early in the morning.

You may continue to plant cucumbers, summer squash and snap peas for fall harvest. Plant potatoes, snapbeans, turnips, winter greens.

Prune hydrangeas that have finished blooming.

Continue to fertilize annuals, perennials and vegetables on a regular schedule.

Continue to look for and treat problems such as aphids and spider mites.

Continue to water regularly and thoroughly. Keep beds weeded and mulched.

SEPTEMBER

Start seeds of hardy annuals now to transplant into the garden in October.

Fall bedding plants, especially chrysanthemums, should be planted now. Plant paperwhite narcissus, snowflakes, Easter lilies, madonna lilies and bearded and Lousianna iris.

Plant fall vegetables such as collards, beets, carrots, mustards, kale, turnips, radishes, lettuce, onions, spinach, parsley and perennial herbs. As in the spring, prepare the beds by digging deeply and adding fertilizer and organic material.

Divide and replant perennials that have finished blooming.

Do only cosmetic pruning of shrubs. You do not want to promote growth that will not mature before cold weather. Remove spent flower heads and seed pods.

Stop fertilizing chrysanthemums when the buds show color. Gerberas and clematis would appreciate a few tablespoons of lime worked into the soil around the base.

September and October tend to be dry months; continue watering regularly.

OCTOBER

Many plants will do better if planted at this time.

Tape a packet of seeds to the October page of your calendar as a reminder. Seeds for perennials, biannuals and hardy annuals should be sown now through November. Root growth will proceed well through winter months. Plants to be put out now include aquilegia, perennial candytuft, dianthus, shasta daisy, hosta, liatris, snapdragons, and pansies. Sweet peas, larkspur and poppies should be sown now for blossoms throughout the spring. Begin planting spring-flowering bulbs. Refrigerate tulips for at least six to eight weeks, but be sure not to refrigerate in the same space with fruits and vegetables. They should be planted in late December or January.

As soon as it cools, begin fall planting of trees and shrubs. Transplant magnolias now.

Divide and transplant daylilies, liriope, ajuga, iris and other perennials as required.

No major pruning is done until early spring.

Fertilize pansies and calendula at planting and three to four weeks later.

To combat scale on camellias and holly, spray with a mixture of oil emulsion and an insecticide. Spraying must be done when daytime temperatures are below eighty-five degrees and night temperatures are above forty degrees.

For a green carpet all winter, the lawn may be overseeded with annual rye grass. Do not fertilize warm-season grasses in the fall.

Keep everything well watered if the fall is dry.

When they finish blooming, hibiscus, allamansa, bird of paradise and other patio plants that are not tolerant of cold weather may be brought into the garage or other sheltered areas for a rest.

NOVEMBER

Trees and shrubs do well when planted in the fall.

Continue planting perennials and hardy annuals. Spring-blooming bulbs may still be planted. Work bone meal into the soil where planting.

Perennials, iris and daylilies may still be divided and transplanted. Divide and transplant dahlias after the first killing frost. They do not require winter storage in our climate.

Pinch back fall-planted snapdragons when they are five inches high. Do this several times for bushier plants. When chrysanthemums have finished blooming, cut back stems to within five inches of the ground.

Check mulch. Its depth should not exceed two inches. Mulch tender plants to protect from cold weather. Remove dead annual plants and cut off the tops of perennials. Keep watering if there is less than an inch of rain each week.

DECEMBER

Tulips may be taken out of the refrigerator and planted this month, or in early January.

It is not too late to plant other spring-flowering bulbs. Hardy annuals and perennials may still be planted.

If a freeze is forecast, water well to prevent damage. Susceptible plants may be covered or heavily mulched, but covering should be removed as it begins to warm, lest further damage occur from rapid warming.

Keep watering.

index

Thanks to Karol DeWulf Nickell for first sending me to produce a story on Savannah gardens in the late 1990s when she was my editor in chief at *Traditional Home*. Now she has assumed that role at *Better Homes and Gardens,* where I am the deputy editor for gardens and outdoor living. Thanks, also, to my friend Jim Darilek, who introduced me to his friend Janice Shay at Design Press, yet another dynamic aspect of the Savannah College of Art and Design. And my appreciation goes to everyone who has helped in the process, from scouting nearly fifty different gardens to sorting out the last details of the index: Cynthia and Eddie DeLoach, editor Gwen Strauss (by delightful coincidence a granddaughter of Fleur Cowles, who inspired my interest in photo-journalism from the time I was in junior high school), gardener Carole Beason, designer Andrea Messina, and, always, Janice and Patrick Shay. Most of all I thank my partner John Zickefoose—a big Daddy Warbucks type and former Chief Steward for the Communications Workers of America, Local 1150, during his days at AT&T —for his impeccable notes and, when pressed, verbatim recall of amusing quotations spoken by cultured Southern lady gardeners. The ability and willingness to make others laugh stands high on my list of admirable behavior.

—Elvin McDonald, West Des Moines, Iowa, June 10, 2003